"Memories on a Plate"

Copyright © 2025 Bob Johnson

Printed in the United States of America
Published by: Writer's Publishing House
Prescott, AZ 86301

Cover Design, Project Management, and Book Launch
by Writers Publishing House

All rights reserved. No part of this book may be reproduced in any manner without written permission from the author except with brief quotations embodied in critical articles and reviews. The fact that an organization or website is referred to in this work as a citation and/or potential source of further information does not mean that the Author or the Publisher endorses the information, the organization, or website it may provide or recommendations it may make. Further, readers should be aware that websites listed in this work may have changed or disappeared between when this work was written and when it was read. Disclaimer: The cases and stories in this book have had details changed to preserve privacy.

Acknowledgements

This **Left Over Ranch** cookbook is made possible through the support of many people I've met along the way, who took the time to teach me about tools and techniques related to food and Leadership. From my first days making classic sandwiches in a Northeast Philadelphia deli, to finally documenting my food journey for others to enjoy 40 years later. There has always been so much to learn, and there always will be- it's been quite a trip!

My deepest thanks to my wife, Carolyn, for her unwavering love, support, and patience as I documented all these recipes and eventually wrote this book. She constantly provided the support and engagement that allowed me to stay focused, always providing valuable feedback and suggestions, along with making and remaking our recipes until they made sense!

A big shout-out to the team at Writer's Publishing House for their hard work in bringing this to life. Special thanks to my editor, Lizzy McNett, whose sharp insights shaped these pages into what they are. Here's to future collaborations and more good times around the table.

Finally, thank you to my readers. You're a big part of my journey. This book is not only about recipes, but also tells the stories behind many of the dishes, my memories on a plate.

Enjoy Reading and Cooking!

Contents

Acknowledgements	2
Introduction	4
Kitchen Essentials	8
The Basics	10
The Playbook	21
Favorites	24
On The Grill	46
Hoagies and Sandwiches	58
Seafood	70
Pork Butt Bonanza	84
Hamamania	96
Pizza and Pasta	105
Chicken and Duck	121
Sides	135
Desserts	159
Category Index	165
Recipe Index	168

The Leftover Ranch Philosophy

The Leftover Ranch philosophy revolves around straightforward principles of food procurement, management, and meal planning, emphasizing opportunistic shopping and minimizing waste. Our approach initially aimed to reduce instances of leftovers going bad due to lack of planning or improper integration into meals. A key aspect of this strategy is embracing flexibility—being open to eating any type of food at any time, regardless of traditional meal categories like "breakfast" or "dinner."

The concept gained momentum when, during a kitchen renovation, I purchased a bucket of fried chicken from a local chain, for the hefty price tag of $37.00 (5 years ago)! This experience highlighted the potential for stretching budget-friendly items as far as possible, and inspired us to share these techniques with others.

Meal Planning

Our first step was to develop the "weekly" or longer meal plan based on two meals a day, since it's hard for us to carve out time to prepare a meal midday, while taking care of the animals and chores around the property. The seven-to-ten-day plan is put together and documented, so we don't end up at 5 o'clock saying "now what are we having for dinner tonight?". The plan is based on what is on hand in the refrigerator, what's left over or nearing its end date, a quick look at the fresh fruit and vegetables (hate to see an avocado go south) on the counter, and which bread products are available fresh or in the freezer. Carolyn maintains a freezer inventory list that is broken out by item, date frozen, and then organized by oldest to newest (and color coded) which hangs on the refrigerator. We maintain a current shopping list in Google lists, which gets updated live time by either of us when working in the kitchen and always includes opportunistic sale items such as pork butt, whole chicken, ham, or ribeye steak.

During meal preparation we utilize a Rachel Ray bowl to capture scraps that either go into the compost pile, which is used on vegetables or trees, or to the chickens and ducks. The last few years we worked on gardens, and even planted some fruit trees, while battling the plethora of hungry animals roving around our property which includes deer, foxes, squirrels, pack rats, javelinas, and a million birds, so now we stick to the grocery or local stands for our produce and meats. I'd rather spend time developing new meals and incorporating them into our playbook.

Culinary Inspirations and Development of my "Point of View"

My original set of recipes were what I would call my **"Memories on a Plate"**, which were based on places I lived, areas I worked in, and people I knew or worked with-experiential. Over the last several years this changed to include development of new dishes based on more recent information and learnings. At this point I had to find a way to group everything into a manageable format and while brainstorming with my wife Carolyn (who also manages our website) we developed the **"Playbook"** approach, since we both come from an operational working background. The Playbook is broken out into twelve sections that provide a standardized and repeatable strategy that support using leftovers, and the "Opportunistic" or "On Sale" approach, since it's hard to walk past a seven-dollar ham or eight-dollar pork shoulder!

My culinary point of view was primarily driven by folks like Emeril Lagasse and more recently Tareq Taylor and Andreas Viestad- basically Southern, Italian and Nordic/Scandinavian which all use similar type ingredients. I grew up in Philadelphia, my stepfather was a Cajun, where I watched Joe Carcione the "Greengrocer" on Channel 6 News, and the "Galloping Gourmet". During high school I worked at Moe's Deli up on Frankford Avenue, where I learned about using quality ingredients and making great sandwiches. Next, I became a produce man at the local market "Farmer's Choice", where I learned about how to identify quality produce (I started out unloading milk trucks and managing the cold box). Once I began working full time, I spent a lot of time in the South Philadelphia neighborhoods and along the Philadelphia waterfront, so I am a big fan of scrapple, pork roll, soft pretzels, creamed chip beef (SOS), Italian grinders, and steak sandwiches (provolone please, wit).

Almost every corner down in South Philly had a sandwich shop and I remember eating pickled pig's feet at 15th and Federal streets early on in my career (it is an acquired taste) and spent lots of time getting to know the "Italian Market" on 9th street. Down near the Delaware river I immersed myself in a multitude of breakfast sandwiches, all on fresh amoroso rolls (which we ship to AZ regularly) and had my favorite lunch/dinner spots like D'Nicks and Tony Luke's on Oregon avenue. Depending on the neighborhood I was in, local cuisine was representative of the culture and heritage in the area- like the E&A Tavern in Port Richmond, who made the best liverwurst and onion sandwich around, or the Schooner Tavern near Old City where mussels in garlic white wine sauce were a staple, along with the senior gentlemen at the bar singing Dean Martin songs...what a great experience and time that was!

Later we lived in Chicagoland, which is when we learned to make our own pizza since we could not get good NY style there or get it "pie cut", and of course made the pilgrimage to "Al's Italian Beef". Next, we moved down near Baltimore and the Chesapeake Bay with its tremendous seafood, Miss Lucy's restaurant, and where we met and spent time with the "Sushi Master" in Bel Air who taught me a lot about integrating flavors from different cuisines together- I think he was the most influential chef I have met since he taught me to think differently about both food and spirituality. We have also had the opportunity to travel and sample local food in England, France, Finland, Germany, Norway, Mexico, and the Netherlands, in small towns and the large cities. All these experiences "molded" my updated culinary point of view and improved our skills for overall food management, preparation, and ultimately taste!

We seldom dine out, choosing instead to refine our own recipes (and we're still mastering sushi). This led us to invest in essential kitchen tools: a stand mixer with a pasta attachment, a meat grinder, and high-quality knives, all recommended by cooking magazines. Over the past decade, we've avidly followed various cooking shows and competitions, read numerous food magazines, and added several cookbooks to our collection. Our approach to leftovers mirrors the "Chopped" style, focusing on creative repurposing, precise knife cuts, presentation, and flavor.

Recently, I was honored with the opportunity to become a Taste of Home Community Cook. We've also expanded our presence online by posting on Instagram (@leftoverranchaz), maintaining our Facebook page (Left Over Ranch), and developing our website, leftoverranch.com. For any inquiries, feel free to reach out to us at leftoverranchaz@gmail.com.

Below are listed the ground rules we use to guide our food journey, lower overall food cost while using fresh ingredients, and limit or eliminate food waste:

1. Use an opportunistic approach of buying things on sale (particularly meats and fish) and figure out how to use/reuse some and freeze the rest for later, so our cost per meal stays way down. Maintain a weekly summary of food related costs, including eating out, then set a target then manage to it. We reward ourselves with sushi when we do well!

2. Create a meal list for the next seven to ten days and shop just for those items, or substitutes, and incorporate the latest updated prioritized freezer inventory. The freezer priority list is color coded with red being for items frozen more than 9 months, and yellow anything more than three months, to ensure the oldest items are being used first.

3. Keep track of the oldest fresh meats and perform a daily produce review, both on the counter and in the refrigerator, into daily meal planning.

4. Do not be tied to "traditional" breakfast or dinner items- Make enough food for dinner that we can have items to repurpose for breakfast or additional dinners.

5. Utilize local and fresh ingredients to make our own mayonnaise and aioles, whipped cream, marinades, sauces, sausage, pizza dough, and pasta. Use fresh horseradish and pickled onions instead of prepared mustard and ketchup and fresh herbs from our "herb wagon".

6. Make our own dessert items like carrot cake, grilled fruit biscuits and whipped cream, key lime pie, apple/peach pie, cookies.

7. Integrate different styles of food type ingredients (Italian, Mexican, Asian, Nordic, Southern, etc.) together to create different taste profiles.

8. Use any waste products to feed our composter or treat the animals (watermelon, tomatoes, red peppers, etc.) and create fresh dirt for reuse.

9. Manage our systems like water use (fill up dog/deer waters to get to hot water), minimize gas use for the stove/oven, and pay close attention to what goes down the drain.

The Leftover Ranch

Carolyn and Titus Batman

Thor, Stripe and Xena

Hagen, the Best Boy, HM, and Nala the Mountain Dog

My Kitchen Essentials

Over the years we have assembled several key tools that are key to making successful meals:

1. The scale, measuring cups/spoons- one of the things I quickly learned when trying to document my recipes was that I needed to have good measurements, for documentation and consistency. The scale comes in very handy when separating pizza dough for calzones and things like that, since it's hard to tell just looking at the pieces.

2. Thermometers-lots of folks talk about wanting to get better at estimating "medium rare" on steaks, personally I go mostly by looks here but for chicken, duck, I use a thermometer. The laser thermometer is a must have when it comes to searing or oil frying in cast iron, so food doesn't turn out oily or get overdone from too high a heat.

3. Knives- and several styles of knives (and my two favorite chef knives) which we sharpen often, before using and after cleaning- "it's a dull knife that hurts you" one of my old bosses used to say. I also have one large, serrated knife we use to cut bread and rolls. The chef knives all get honed about once a year, it's well worth the effort.

4. Cutting boards-we have several sizes of plastic and rubber boards that get used daily and can drop right in the dishwasher. For larger items like ham, roast chicken, or cutting pizza, I have two nice size wooden boards. Don't forget the pizza peel which hangs out with the wooden boards!

5. The Roasting Pan- it's been with us for many years and is used for baking ham, and roasting whole chicken, with internal removable rack that makes cleaning a snap.

6. Our Dutch ovens by Lodge, in two sizes "large" and "small" (I can't read the bottom), are perfect for braising beef shanks and duck legs or making soups, stews, stocks, and mac and cheese.

7. The stand mixer- I don't know how we survived without this tool! It's a great one-time investment that supports all kinds of meals, condiments, bread, and pizza dough and more.

8. The hand or emulsion blender is great for small amounts of mayonnaise, making sauces, and processing things like chipotles, or making duck liver mousse.

9. My rolling mat, which provides a great surface to work on, along with measurements on it for better consistency and we use several styles of rolling pins depending on the meal.

10. The meat grinder is another one-time investment that helps with things like on sale pork shoulder (think breakfast sausage and ground meats), that can be frozen for another day and are so much better homemade.

11. Baking dishes-we have two glass "Pyrex" dishes two and three quart, that are years old, and a few ceramic/steel ones that came out of a basement at 24th and South in Philly. I use them a lot for reheating leftovers and roasting chicken wings.

12. Favorite pots and pans- again several of my favorite pots and pans came out of the same basement at 24th and South Street, we recently picked up a set of copper nonstick pans, really like them. I do have 1 stainless steel pan that only gets used for bacon, and two very wide Rachel R ay pans for omelets, duck fat potatoes and heating Italian rolls.

13. Cast Iron Pans-our kitchen has eight cast iron pans (all Lodge) that run from 5 -12 inches in diameter, one that's very deep I use to sear garlic shrimp, one flat for heating tortillas, and weight for rolls. Anything that needs searing like tuna or scallops goes into cast iron, as well as baking like pasta pie or cornbread, just can't say enough about how they hold the heat and are great on the grill as well. In fact, my new pizza stone is made by Lodge, has great handles, and works perfectly!

14. My pizza stone journey- over the years we have tried many different pizza stones, moving from heating "Boboli" crusts 20 years ago to making our own while living in Chicago. We moved from thin steel, up to a real stone, next to "Pizza Steel" that weighed 16 pounds and had no handles, and finally to the Lodge cast iron "stone" that is just perfect, easy to manipulate, great heat transfer, and quick clean up.

15. The Grill- My grill is an old Weber "Spirit" that we've had for about 15 years now, I just keep rebuilding it every few years, or change out worn out parts. It's not fancy but I understand how it heats, it's very well-seasoned, and with three burners I can turn one off and do some quick Juniper smoking (since we are in a Juniper Forest).

16. Finally, we have a good assortment of metal bowls, whisks, wooden and plastic spoons, spatulas, and graters since we like to grate our own cheeses and horseradish.

The Basics-Condiment Corner

This section lists out the items that we keep on hand at all times- some are store bought, some are other Chef's recipes that we use, and the rest we developed and make ourselves including:

- "Johnsons Barbeque Sauce" which we developed after reviewing other Instagram user's recipes, and incorporated ingredients we like.

- "Revamped Russian Dressing" which incorporates our Southwest point of view and is awesome on pastrami Reubens.

- "Pickled Beet Eggs", a traditional Pennsylvania favorite great for breakfast in a hurry.

- "Pickled Onions and Jalapenos" a Scandinavian profile that replaces several other condiments.

- "Homemade Stock" of all types that start with the same base and has only fresh ingredients.

- "Brandy Whipped Cream" is really hard to beat, especially on grilled fruit.

- "Poached Eggs" perfect with potato pancakes, latkes, and duck fat potatoes.

Over the last several years of our food journey, we've tried many new ideas for things like mayonnaise, hot sauce, mustard, etc. that support many of our dishes, and finally landed on a set group of items we make ourselves, and those we buy already made because its less expensive and tastes just fine, and I am always looking for new things to add, like oyster sauce— just started using it this winter!

Crushed Chipotle in Adobo Sauce

We really enjoy the taste and mild heat of chipotle peppers, the whole peppers in adobo sauce are nice but hard to cut up and messy. I used to be able to find them ground at the store, but not very often these days, so now I just pick up a can of La Costena chipotles, drop in a bowl and grind with an immersion blender, then store in a mason jar in the refrigerator-much easier and less cost.

Fresno Pepper Hot Sauce

I found this fermented pepper hot sauce recipe in "Cook's Country" magazine Dec/Jan 2020 edition written by Matthew Fairman, which we always have on hand, stored in a small mason jar on the fridge door. The depth of flavor and mild heat adds just enough kick to many dishes without the vinegar bite associated with many hot sauces.

Helen Rennie's Magic Sauce

Some of our favorite Asian food types are sushi, sashimi, tuna loin, and lions head meatballs-can't get enough of it. One day while watching YouTube we came across Helen Rennie teaching how to make her "Soy Reduction aka The Magic Sauce", based on Tamari, Bonita flakes, Kombu, and shiitake mushrooms, which is a perfect garnish for all types of dishes. I always have a squeeze bottle in the refrigerator, ready to go.

Chimichurri

Whenever we make "on sale" London broil or steaks, I normally use our homemade barbeque sauce, but it's nice to take a break and use Mirta's (Mirta Rinaldi) chimichurri recipe I found in "Food and Wine" September 2021 edition, its fresh and light, can be used in lots of applications, and lasts a couple of weeks in the refrigerator.

Mustard

Over the years we've gone round and round on mustard types, for most of my life Guldens was it for Philadelphia soft pretzels, and horseradish mustard worked on most other dishes. Once we started making our own and tinkering with that, which became expensive to make and usually hit or miss, we decided to just use store bought Dijon, like Grey Poupon.

Wines

My all-around favorite cooking wine is Marsala, it adds a ton of flavor to many of our vegetable dishes, or" Yellow Tail "white wine for a few dishes, Sake for sushi rice and Asian vegetable dishes.

Hot Sauces

Besides the Fresno pepper hot sauce used for cooking, we also use a few others, specifically:

- "Louisiana" Hot Sauce- kept in a squeeze bottle, is perfect for eggs in the morning and fried chicken prep.
- "Tabasco" Chipotle Hot Sauce- just found this recently in Tucson great on omelets and southwest dishes.
- "Old Bay" Hot Sauce- it's an absolutely fantastic taste which we use for chicken salad, crabcake aioles, and similar dishes.
- "Franks" Hot Sauce- use this along with homemade barbeque sauce for wings and on my fries.
- Gochujang- this goes into all my Asian vegetable and/or meat dishes, it's just awesome.
- Worchester Sauce- while not a "hot sauce" After seeing a YouTube video on how Worcestershire is made, I really like using it when I can, nice depth of flavor.

Oils

We primarily use three types of oil, kept in Rachel Ray decanters on our countertop- Olive oil, Peanut oil, and Avocado oil, depending on what type of dish and the heat required to make it, peanut for fried chicken, fish and chips, or French fries, and avocado oil spray for most pan oiling. I use rendered duck fat for potatoes and latkes, there is nothing else like it. I try to keep butter to a minimum, mainly for grilling bread for sandwiches. We've recently started using beef tallow in several of our dishes , including steak fries, which is all natural.

Vinegars

I'm not a big fan of white vinegar, too much bite, we normally use apple cider vinegar for most applications, red wine vinegar on tomatoes for grinders and calzones, malt vinegar with fish and chips, white balsamic wherever balsamic is needed, and finally rice vinegar for cucumber salad, sushi rice sticks, and many other dishes.

Everything Else

Like most folks we also keep lots of other things on hand in the cabinet, depending on the flavor profile of the dish we want to create, like mirin, miso, sesame oil, etc. I try to go with our favorites but am always looking to try new things and do more fusion.

Mayonnaise And Aioles

Our mayonnaise recipe is inspired by Celebrity Swedish Cooking Chef Tareq Taylor- it's simple and tastes great- the trick is to pour the oil in so slow that it hurts!

Ingredients

- 2 duck or chicken egg yolks
- 1 tbsp Dijon mustard
- 1 tbsp apple cider vinegar
- Pinch of salt
- 1 ¼ cup avocado oil

1. Whisk to combine egg yolks, mustard, apple cider vinegar and salt into a mixing bowl. A stand mixer at medium speed is my choice for making an emulsion like mayonnaise. An immersion blender, hand mixer or whisk can also be used instead of the stand mixer.

2. Add the oil to the bowl in a small steady stream, as slowly as possible, while whisking/mixing. It takes me about 8-10 minutes to add all the oil.

3. Use immediately or scoop into a mason jar and refrigerate for later.

4. Combine 1 -2 tbsp of mayonnaise with 1 tsp of chopped chipotles with adobo and a splash of lime juice for BLTs.

5. Combine 3 tbsp of mayonnaise with ½ tsp cardamom or coriander and thin with lemon juice to a nice sauce consistency for use on fish, crabcakes, and shrimp tacos.

Brandy Whipped Cream

Whenever we would look for whipped cream at the supermarket, the labels normally stated "flavoring" or other non-natural ingredients, so we started looking into making our own at home. After a few tries we landed on this version, which is super easy and can be enhanced with any personal favorite ingredient.

Ingredients

- 1 cup heavy cream
- 1 tsp vanilla extract
- 2 tbsp confectioners' sugar
- 2 tsp Brandy

1. Place metal mixing bowl and whisk attachment in the freezer for 10-15 minutes. Make sure the heavy cream is kept cold.
2. Put the heavy cream, vanilla extract, confectioners' sugar, and brandy into the cold bowl.
3. Whisk the ingredients together on medium-high speed until peaks form. Stop whisking before the peaks become too stiff. The peaks should stand up and curl slightly at the top.
4. Serve immediately, can last a few days in the refrigerator.

Johnson's Barbeque Sauce

We have tried many commercial barbeque sauces, but they all have too much sugar and many lack flavor. The sponsor of an Instagram group I belong to shared her Texas recipe, too hot for us, but I used her philosophy to develop my own sauce! It's a great all-around sauce that I use for many dishes, not only barbeque.

Ingredients

15 oz tomato sauce

¼ cup Bourbon

¼ cup apple cider vinegar

½ cup local honey

1 tbsp Worcestershire

1 tsp chili powder

2 tbsp Dijon mustard

1 tsp cayenne powder

2 tsp dark brown sugar

2 tsp molasses

3 cloves garlic minced

1 shallot minced

1. Mix all the listed ingredients together and bring to a boil, then simmer for 8-10 minutes or until about 20% reduced.
2. Pour into a clean Mason jar and store in the refrigerator.

Revamped Russian Dressing

Years ago, when I was working at Moe's Deli up on Frankford Avenue, we'd make all kinds of sandwiches, including Reubens and "Specials" with corned beef or pastrami. One ingredient of those sandwiches, "Russian Dressing", fell out of favor over the years- you can't even find it in the market anymore. This sauce is all natural and packs a real punch of flavor!

Ingredients

- 2 tsp brown sugar
- 2 tsp celery seed
- 1 tsp smoked paprika
- 4 tsp lemon juice
- 4 tsp Worcestershire
- 1 tsp molasses
- 2 tbsp apple cider vinegar
- 8 oz tomato sauce
- ¼ cup shallot, finely chopped
- 2 tsp chopped/crushed chipotle with adobo sauce

1. Combine all the ingredients in a small saucepan, stir well, and bring to a boil. Reduce the heat to a medium simmer for about 10 minutes, then transfer to a small mason jar. This lasts about three weeks in the refrigerator.

Homemade Stock

Making stock at home is super easy and allows for different variations to meet our cooking needs. We started making our own after watching Andreas Viestad make his duck stock. Making homemade saves money, uses leftover ingredients so nothing goes to waste, and contains less salt and preservatives than store-bought.

Ingredients

- 1 large or 2 medium carrots peeled and chopped
- 2 large stalks celery chopped
- ½ yellow onion chopped
- ½ small leek chopped (Optional)
- 8 cups water (minimum)
- 2-3 Bay leaves
- 2 tsp olive oil
- ½ tsp ground Himalayan salt (or Icelandic)
- ½ tsp fresh ground pepper
- Protein if desired

1. Drop the olive oil in a Dutch oven and start to heat at medium. Next add the vegetables and allow to cook (stirring often) until they become fragrant, then add the water and bay leaf, (add the protein here if desired) stirring to combine.

2. Turn the heat up to get a good boil going then reduce to medium again, add the salt and pepper, and allow to reduce down about 50% (between 45-60 minutes).

3. Remove the large pieces with a slotted spoon, then strain into a quart measuring cup. Taste and adjust salt/pepper to taste. Ready for use in risotto and other dishes warm.

4. Pour into a clean mason jar, place the lid on and store in the refrigerator for up to two weeks, or can be placed in airtight containers and frozen.

5. Chicken wing tips, necks, and giblets, duck necks and giblets, shellfish shells, and other leftover protein bits can be added to make different flavoured broths.

6. Depending on the meals I am planning I may add more water than the 8 cups.

Poached Eggs

We really enjoy the poached eggs in our local Diner's eggs benedict, so I started making poached eggs at home, since they are quick and easy, and use up our chicken's eggs. It just takes a little practice to consistently get runny yolks, the key is to monitor them and not rely only on time.

Ingredients

- 4 large eggs
- 3 tbsp apple cider vinegar
- ¼ tsp salt
- Salt and pepper to taste
- 8-12 cups water
- Hot sauce of choice (We like to use Old Bay or Louisiana hot sauce)

1. In a deep saucepan add the water, vinegar, and salt then place on the lid. Stir well and bring to a boil, then set to a very low boil and keep covered.
2. Crack each egg into ramekins or similar small container (bowls/cups), send the shells to the compost.
3. Remove the lid on the pan, and give the water/vinegar solution a light "swirl", then gently place each egg in by holding the container in the water first, then gently allowing the egg to go in. Once the eggs are all in, replace the lid, and set the timer for 3 minutes.
4. Check again in about a minute to confirm the water is still at a low boil, adjust as necessary.
5. At or near three minutes (somewhere between 2 and 3) remove the cover, the eggs should be starting to float, remove them with a slotted spoon, drain on the spoon on a towel or napkin, then they are ready to plate and add salt and pepper to taste.
6. These are great on potato pancakes, home fries, or duck fat potatoes.

Beet Pickled Eggs

Growing up in and around Philadelphia, one of our favorite snacks was beet pickled eggs, especially along with some cottage cheese and salt and pepper. It's a Pennsylvania Dutch classic! We make these just about every week, and would normally steam and then use a cold-water bath. Carolyn now uses our new air fryer to hard-boiled eggs, it's much easier, takes less time, and saves propane gas.

Ingredients

- 6 large eggs
- 15 oz can sliced beets in water (not pickled) with juice reserved
- ½ onion cut in small thin strips
- 1 jalapeno cored and chopped
- ½ cup sugar
- ½ cup apple cider vinegar
- 2 allspice berries
- 2 cloves
- ¼ Tsp Salt
- ¼ tsp pepper

1. Because fresh eggs are so hard to peel, I hard boil eggs using an air fryer for 15 minutes at 275 °F.
2. Combine the reserved beet juice, onion, sugar, jalapeno, apple cider vinegar, allspice, cloves, salt, pepper and bring to a boil on medium high heat.
3. Lower heat and simmer/boil for 10 minutes.
4. Allow the liquid to cool. Remove the allspice berries and cloves from the liquid with tongs.
5. Place two peeled eggs in the bottom of a 1-quart mason jar, with ⅓ of the beets and ⅓ third of the liquid with onions. Repeat the layering two times. Screw on the lid and place in the refrigerator. The eggs will be ready to eat the next day.

Pickled Onions & Jalapenos

These quick pickled vegetables are a great replacement for store bought condiments. They add a nice flavor and crunch to lots for dishes from chorizo burgers to our E&A sandwich, and are inspired by New Scandinavian Cooking's Tareq Taylor.

Ingredients

- ½ large red onion sliced thin and halved
- 1 large jalapeno cored and sliced
- ⅓ cup apple cider vinegar
- ¼ cup organic raw cane sugar
- ½ cup water
- ½ apple cored, peeled, sliced (Optional)

1. Whisk the apple cider vinegar, sugar, and water together until the sugar dissolves, then add the sliced red onions and sliced jalapenos. Let stand for 30-60 minutes stirring several times before serving.
2. Apples can be added to this mixture for use with barbequed pork sandwiches, with ham or on pizza.

The Playbook

Now that we've gone through our Introduction, Essential Tools, and the Basics, I'd like to discuss how the "Playbook" was put together.

For many years I had a set of recipes in my mind that I would make, and finally started to write them down in an old spiral notebook. Early on there were only ingredients listed and some rudimentary steps, but no measurements or temperatures, not even good cooking times. Once we decided to start documenting these recipes, I would make each one, capturing everything I did during preparation, then take pictures of the start ingredients and final dish. Carolyn would then make it and give me feedback. We'd make the dish again (or more) until it was clear and repeatable. Most of the dishes are written and prepared for two, several with great leftovers.

As the individual recipes started coming together, they had to be categorized- since we both came from operational backgrounds it made sense to group things by how we how we manage our meal planning. This was my "aha" moment which then turned into the 12 Playbook categories, so I could finally prioritize and organize the list.

Here's a quick synopsis of each:

Favorites: These are dishes we make often, from my first food memory, Grandma Tate's Potato Pancakes, then travel through time with things I've eaten over the years. The last thing we integrated recently are Duck Fat Potato and Chorizo crispy tacos, which are inspired by a small restaurant in Glendale, Arizona.

Grill: Everything tastes better cooked on a well-seasoned grill! I use our grill during all seasons and in all weather, even rain or snow, and use juniper chips from the forest we live in for extra flavor and or smoking. Our grill is a 13-year-old Weber Spirit that gets its internal parts rebuilt every few years, instead of buying new.

Rolls (Hoagies and Sandwiches): Most of these come from my Delaware riverfront experiences, where lots of small "mom and pop" shops made any sandwich you requested on a fresh Amoroso hoagie roll, with hot cherry peppers on the side. We ship in Amoroso rolls from the East Coast throughout the year. The term "hoagie" came from when small shops sold this type of sandwich to shipyard workers who went to Hog Island to work in the early 1900s.

The Playbook

Seafood: Classic revised dishes based on things I ate as a kid in Jersey or on the waterfront, like crab stuffed lobster, or dover sole from England. What isn't included are some Eastern Shore favorites, like soft shell crabs, oysters, Arctic char, that we can't get out here.

Pork Butt Bonanza: Once we find an on-sale pork shoulder (commonly called the Boston Butt), it's immediately broken down into 1–2-pound blocks, with the remaining items used for our breakfast sausage, which supports meatloaf, meatballs, and my favorite, biscuits, and gravy. What doesn't get used right away gets frozen and added to the inventory.

Hamamania: We always pick up a couple "on-sale" hams after holidays, which is what really started us documenting how to stretch an item as far as possible to lower costs. The $13 dollar ham challenge shows how we committed to only using what was in the house, along with the ham, and got 12-13 meals. Didn't shop again all week!

Pizza and Pasta: All pizzas and calzones are made with our homemade dough and have been tailored to fit our taste and use San Marzano tomatoes. After lots of trial and error, we now only use a Lodge pizza pan, nice handles and great weight.

Chicken and Duck: Whenever chicken or duck goes on sale, I'll pick a couple up and well run through some recipes in this section. Normally, I'll roast chicken, with a rice side and quick sauce (I keep frozen cranberries and cherries in the freezer year-round), then use the rest for leftovers. Necks and internals are used for stock and duck liver mousse.

Sides: We eat a lot of rice and combine it with all types of other fresh vegetables and flavors, especially things like grilled corn, grilled pineapple, and my personal favorite roasted okra - looking to always use fresh ingredients and make plenty for leftovers.

Desserts: We only make a few desserts, mainly with frilled fruit, or caramelized nuts, and my 1700's version of rice pudding, never having the chance to get my Grandma Tates recipe, which she made in the old double boiler.

Other Recipes We Use: I have another binder for recipes we like from magazines, the internet, cooking shows, and Taste of Home which is part of my community cook responsibilities.

The Playbook

1	Background	LOR Revised Background									
2	Key Tools	Cast Iron Pans	Scale	Meat Grinder	Pizza Stone	Dutch Oven	Roasting Pan	Stand mixer	Rolling matt and pins	Baking Dishes	Hand Blender
3	Basics 3A - Condiment Corner Breakout	3B - Mayo and Aioli	3C - Whipped Cream	3D - Johnson's BBQ Sauce	3E - Revamped Russian Dressing	3F - Stock	3G - Poached Eggs	3H - Pickled Beet Eggs	3I - Pickled Onions & Peppers		
4	Favorites	4A - Grandma Tate's Potato Cakes	4B - Southland French Toast	4C - High Desert Omelet	4D - The E&A	4E - Pastrami Reuben	4F - Earthy Omelet	4G - Flightline Nachos	4H - All Day BLT	4I - Cast Iron Stir Fry	4J - Pork Medallions
		4K - Braised Shanks	4L - Cream Chipped Beef (SOS)	4M - BJ's Capri Salad	4N - Pickled Grilled Cheese	4O - LO RIB Fajitas	4P - Saddle Butte Perogies	4Q - South Street Perogies	4R - LO Steak Fajitas	4S - Hilltop Haluski	4T - Crispy Potato Chorizo Tacos
5	Grill	5A - Prospector Burger (Nordic)	5B - Ranch Hand Burger (SW)	5C - Brandy Grilled Pineapple	5D - Grilled Corn	5E - BBQ Grilled Game Hens	5F - Country Style Ribs	5G - Grilled Ribeye Steak	5H - Juniper Smoked Duck Breast	5I - BBQ Smoked Salmon	5J - Marinated Pork Chops Plum Chutney
6	Hoagies and Sandwiches (Rolls)	6A - Two Street Grinder	6B - Delaware and Oregon - Pork Roll Egg & Cheese	6C - Schuylkill Station Scrapple, Egg & Cheese	6D - Roast Beef and Fried Onion Hoagie	6E - Garlic Chicken Cheese Steak Sandwich	6F - Hot Roast Beef Mozzarella Sandwich	6G - Tailgate Tribute - Brats	6H - Duke's Meatball Sandwich	6I - Front Street Steak Sandwich	6J - Phil's Pepperoni Pizza Steak
		6K - Left Over Rib Sandwich									
7	Seafood	7A - First Mate's Crab Stuffed Shrimp	7B - New Iberia Shrimp and Andouille	7C - Xen Tuna Loin and Rice Sticks	7D - Inner Harbor Crab Cakes	7E - Garlic Shrimp Tacos	7F - Western Seared Scallops	7G - Cast Iron BBQ Shrimp	7H - Shrimp and Okra Hoagie	7I - Chesapeake Fried Green Tomatoes	7J - The Queen's Fish and Chips
		7K - Flat Fish Fry	7L - Seared Squid								
8	Pork Shoulder	8A - Pork Butt Bonanza (Based on $8 pork butt)	8B - BJ's Ground Pork	8C - 10th Street Pork Sandwich	8D - Lions Head Meatballs	8E - The Southwark Sausage Egg and Cheese	8F - JB's Meatballs and Red Sauce	8G - Mountainview Meatloaf and Leftovers	8H - Biscuits and Gravy	8I - 8 Minute Egg Rolls	
9	Ham	9A - Whole Ham $13	9B - Chipotle Honey Mustard Sauce	9C - Ham Egg and Cheese	9D - HLT (HELT) eggs	9E - Grilled Ham Avocado Sandwich	9F - Ham Pizza Onions & Apples	9G - Jalapeno Mac and Cheese	9H - Ham Mac & Cheese Pizza	9I - Mac and Cheese Fajita	9J - Corn Chowder
10	Pizza and Pasta	10 - Pizza Dough	10B - Make Ahead Pasta Sauce	10C - Green Tomato Pizza	10D - Napoli Pizza	10E - Spinach and Garlic White Pizza	10F - Spanish Chorizo Cotija Pizza	10G - Pasta Pie	10H - Oiled Spinach and Mushroom Pasta	10I - Pasta Refresh	10J - Spinach and Mushroom Manicotti
		10K - CJ's Travel Lasagna	10L - Pasta Salad	10M - Catch All Calzone							
11	Chicken and Duck	11A - LOR Chicken Story	11B - Old Bay Chicken Corn Salad Sandwich	11C - Quick Chicken Fajita	11D - BBQ Chicken Pizza	11E - Buffalo Blue Cheese Chicken Salad Hoagie	11F - Buffalo BBQ Calzone	11G - Buffalo Barbeque Wings	11H - LO Chicken Hand Pies	11I - LOR Duck Story	11J - Rendered Duck Fat
12	Sides	12A - Edna's Sauerkraut	12B - BJ's Duck Fat Potatoes	12C - Kathryn's Baked Beans	12D - Roasted Okra	12E - Avocado Corn Salsa	12F - Desert Dirty Rice	12G - Ginger Rice	12H - Vegetable Corn Rice	12I - Honey Chipotle Apples and Onions	12J - Western Mushy Peas
		12K - Nordic Mashed Roots	12L - Pea Spinach Risotto	12M - Grilled Baked Potato	12N - Russet and Sweet Potato Fries	12O - Japanese Cucumber salad	12P - Garden Vegetable Orzo	12Q - BBQ Fried Brussels	12R - Braised Green Beans	12S - Carolyn's Creamed Spinach	12T - DB's Candied Carrots
		12U - Coconut Rice									
13	Desserts	13A - Rice Pudding	13B - Cherry Vanilla Clafoutis	13C - Marinated Grilled Peaches	13D - Candied Pecans and Peanuts	13E - Apple and Pear Pie with Crumble Top					

Uncle "Pap" SSGT James Brown

CWO Dewey Alford Tate

Favorites

Dewey A. Tate Jr. "Uncle Buddy" and me 1966

Francis Marion Tate, "Grandma Tate"

24   Leftover Ranch

Grandma Tate's Potato Pancakes

One of my first food memories was in my grandmother's Philadelphia rowhouse kitchen, while she was making potato pancakes from left over mashed potatoes. She would make a patty out of a ball of potatoes, dip them in flour and cook in a cast iron pan with melted butter. Over the years I've taken that concept and updated it with my own point of view, added poached eggs, and hot sauce!

Ingredients

- Left over mashed root vegetables or mashed potatoes
- 1 large jalapeno finely chopped
- ½ large onion finely chopped
- ½ tsp Old Bay seasoning
- ½ cup corn meal
- ¼ cup AP flour
- ¼ cup Panko breadcrumbs
- 4 eggs out of the shell (Chicken)
- 1 egg beaten (optional)
- 3 tbsp apple cider vinegar
- 2 tsp Tabasco Chipotle hot sauce (or personal favorite)
- 2 tbsp butter
- Celery/parsley leaves

1. In a large wide pot filled 4/5ths to the top with water add the apple cider vinegar and ½ tsp of salt, bring to a low boil covered and set heat to maintain. Place the eggs in separate ramekins or small bowls.
2. Use a large spoon to measure out four meatball sized lumps of mashed root vegetables and place in metal bowl. Add the chopped jalapenos and onions, mix to combine, then make four balls. If the mash is very dry add the beaten egg.
3. On a flat plate mix the corn meal, flour, breadcrumbs, old bay, and salt/pepper with a fork, then roll the root vegetable balls through it to coat thoroughly.
4. Melt the butter on a non-stick griddle on medium heat, then place the pancake "balls" on it and lightly "smash" them down. Allow to cook until the bottom starts to brown then carefully flip over and brown the other side. Place two pancakes on each plate.
5. While the pancakes are cooking, reconfirm the low boil is still going in the pot, swirl the water, then gently add the four eggs into the boiling water they take between 2-3 minutes. Once the eggs start to transform and float, I pull them out with a serrated spoon, drain the water, and add one on top of each pancake. Add chopped celery leaves or parsley, salt and pepper to taste, garnish with hot sauce.

Southland French Toast

Whenever I have a partial Italian/French bread loaf around, I like to make a sweet and spicy French Toast dish that includes one of several fruits usually around the kitchen like blueberries or raspberries, or any grilled fruit like pears, peaches, or plums. I place the syrup in a ramekin for dipping and make the fruit the star of the dish.

Ingredients

Toast

- Four ¾" to 1" pieces of Italian or French bread
- 3 eggs (duck or chicken)
- 4 oz half and half
- ½ tsp cinnamon
- ½ tsp cayenne
- ½ tsp vanilla extract
- Juice from 1 large orange or 2 clementines
- 2 oz butter
- 4 oz maple syrup

Fruit Options

- 12 oz fresh blueberries or raspberries
- 3 small previously marinated and grilled peaches or pears (usually marinated in brown sugar, olive oil, bourbon/brandy, fermented hot sauce)
- 2 oranges peeled and sliced combined with ¼ tsp brown sugar
- Sauteed apples

1. Whisk together the eggs, half and half, cinnamon, cayenne, vanilla, and orange juice then set aside. Mix again just prior to use.
2. On a griddle melt the butter and spread around evenly- submerge each bread slice in the egg mixture and turn several times to soak it. Place on the griddle and cook until brown, turning several times.
3. Place two pieces of toast on each plate, add your preferred fruit topping (if using previously grilled fruit from the refrigerator heat on the griddle first), and pour natural/organic maple syrup around the outside of each piece of bread or place in a ramekin for dipping.
4. Feel free to add any breakfast meat of choice, my favorite with this dish is scrapple!

High Desert Omelet

This dish was originally developed as a use for left over taco components like broken shells, meat, cheese and cut vegetables. Over time it morphed into a version of chorizo and eggs, combined with vegetables that are quick pickled in white balsamic vinegar, and includes a chipotle/lime sour cream instead of cheese.

1. Finely chop the onion, jalapeno, tomatoes; mix in bowl with the balsamic. Stir occasionally, season with salt and pepper before serving.

2. Cut avocado into four long pieces, slice, place on each plate. Squeeze 1/2 lime juice over, add salt and pepper. Place two tostadas per plate beside avocado.

3. In oiled cast iron or stainless pan, cook chorizo until done. Add the corn kernels and cook until the corn becomes fragrant, then turn off heat.

4. Whisk the eggs and half-and-half, pour into lightly oiled non-stick pan. Cook on medium until set. Mix sour cream, chipotle, 1/2 lime juice in a bowl.

5. Spoon chorizo/corn mixture down omelet center, add chipotle lime sour cream. Fold sides over, cut in half. Place omelet halves on tostadas, top with onion, jalapeno and tomato mixture using a slotted spoon, garnish with cilantro.

Ingredients

- 4 Tostadas Nortenas Clasicas
- 4 oz fresh chorizo
- 1 ear roasted corn kernels (or equivalent canned corn)
- 1 medium-large avocado
- 1 lime halved
- ½ large white or yellow onion
- 1 large jalapeno
- 2 roma tomatoes (or 1 large red tomato) cored
- ¼ cup white balsamic vinegar
- 2-3 tbsp sour cream
- 1 tsp crushed chipotle In adobo sauce
- 3-4 fresh eggs
- ¼ cup half & half
- Avocado oil spray
- Cilantro

Favorites 27

The "E&A" Sandwich

Back in the day we would eat lunch at local restaurants along the riverfront in Philly, near the generating stations we maintained. On the North side, the E&A Tavern made the best and thickest liverwurst and onion sandwiches in town. This dish is inspired by that sandwich using Braunschweiger, pickled onions and jalapenos, Jewish rye, Dijon mustard, and Swiss cheese to create a "European Cubano" style sandwich.

Ingredients

- 8 oz Braunschweiger sausage sliced into 4 pieces and cut in half
- 4 slices Jewish rye bread
- 1 jalapeno sliced and cored
- ½ yellow onion sliced
- ⅓ cup apple cider vinegar
- ⅓ cup water
- ¼ cup sugar
- 2 tbsp Dijon mustard
- 4-6 slices Swiss cheese
- 2 tbsp butter
- Pickle slices for garnish

1. Combine the apple cider, water, and sugar and mix thoroughly, then add the onions and jalapenos and allow to marinate for about 30 minutes or longer. Stir several times.

2. Melt the butter on a grill pan and lay the 4 slices of bread down, browning the first side, flip over and lightly brown the other side. Turn down the heat and move the bread to a board or plate.

3. On the browned side of two pieces of bread, lay on the Braunschweiger and smash down with a fork, followed by a layer of cheese, onions and jalapenos, and another layer of cheese. Spread Dijon mustard on the two remaining slices and top each sandwich.

4. Place the sandwiches back on the griddle, and press down with a cast iron pan, turn the heat to medium to brown the bottom for a couple minutes, then turn the pan upside down and cover so the cheese melts. Once the cheese is melted remove from the griddle and plate, cut in half, then add your favorite garnish and serve.

Mountain Guide's Reuben

My original training on making deli sandwiches came from my time working at Moe's Deli, on Frankford Avenue above Cottman, in the 1970s. It was my second real job and the woman who ran the deli had very high standards for ingredients and our performance. Her teachings are the inspiration for this sandwich, and several others, which uses homemade Russian dressing with only natural ingredients.

Ingredients

- 2-3 tbsp "Revamped Russian Dressing" from the "Basic's" Section.
- 4 slices Jewish rye bread
- 6 slices baby Swiss cheese
- ½ lb pastrami sliced thin
- ½ large yellow/white onion
- 1 large jalapeno cored and chopped
- 6-8 oz fermented cabbage or store bought Saur Kraut
- 2 tbsp butter
- 2 tbsp olive oil
- Olives for garnish

1. Rinse the Saur kraut (no need to rinse the fermented cabbage) and then sauté in 1 tbsp oil in non-stick pan until its starts to dry out. Add the onion and jalapeno and remaining oil, let cook till onions are translucent stirring frequently.

2. While the Saur kraut is cooking, on a griddle melt the butter and brown the bread on both sides. Place three slices of Swiss cheese and half the pastrami on two of the slices, remove to the plates and turn off the griddle. (leave remaining rye bread there for now).

3. Next spoon some Revamped Russian dressing over the pastrami, followed by the Saur kraut/onion/jalapeno mixture, then place the remaining rye bread slices on top. Sprinkle with salt and pepper, cut each sandwich in half, and add olives of choice to the dish.

Earthy Omelet

We normally have plenty of eggs from our chickens and I'm always looking to make something with them and use up any partial ingredients hanging around, like half a carton of mushrooms, partial container of spinach, and those last few pieces of baby Swiss cheese. Putting this all together into an omelet, along with a side of Jewish rye and pork roll, reminds me of heading out to the Mayfair diner back in the day.

Ingredients

- 8 oz mushrooms (any kind on hand)
- 2 large handfuls of spinach
- 3 –4 eggs
- ¼ cup half and half
- 2 tbsp marsala wine
- 1 large shallot chopped
- 1 tbsp fresh grated horseradish
- 3 garlic cloves chopped
- 2-3 slices baby Swiss cheese
- ½ lemon
- 2 tbsp olive oil
- Avocado oil spray

1. In a mixing bowl whisk the eggs and half and half until smooth and set aside. Mix this one last time just before cooking.
2. In a deep non-stick pan heat up the olive oil, add the shallots and mushrooms, and cook for a few minutes, add salt and pepper to taste, then cook until they start to give off water.
3. Next pour in the cooking wine, drop in the spinach and garlic and cover. Allow this to cook undisturbed for 2-3 minutes, then remove the lid and stir. Continue to cook on medium heat until the spinach just starts to break down. Start heating up the omelet pan sprayed with avocado oil.
4. Once the omelet pan is hot, pour in the eggs and cook until they harden up. Next lay the mushroom spinach mixture along the center, followed by the horseradish, then lay on the cheese. Fold both sides of the egg over the center. Cut this in half, move it to plates, and squeeze fresh lemon juice over top.
5. I usually add a piece or two of grilled sourdough or rye bread to round out the dish.

Flightline Nachos

The first time I landed at Marine Corps Air Station Yuma, Arizona, locals took us to a restaurant serving massive sheet-pan nachos—unlike anything on the East Coast. I've since tweaked the recipe, adding more cheeses, homemade fried tortillas, refried beans, and fresh avocado. Grilled corn pairs perfectly.

Ingredients

- 5-6 yellow corn tortillas (6-Inch)
- 8 oz Rosarita spicy jalapeno refried beans (or similar)
- 2 medium avocados
- 1 large jalapeno sliced cored and chopped
- 8 oz fresh chorizo
- 1.5 oz cheddar cheese grated
- 1.5 oz pepper jack cheese grated
- 1.5 oz Cotija cheese crumbled
- 1 lime halved
- Cilantro for garnish
- Peanut oil (enough for about ½ inch in the pan)

1. Cut the tortillas into quarters, then heat about ½ inch peanut oil in a cast iron or similar skillet (we use a 9.5 inch for this) to between 375 and 400 °F. Drop in a few tortilla pieces and flip once while cooking, this does not take long so don't let them burn! Pull from the oil and place on rack set in a large sheet pan.

2. Drop the chorizo into a pan at medium low heat and allow it to cook down, moving it around often, for about 8 minutes then turn off the heat. While the chorizo is cooking cut the avocados into 4 sections longways, peel and remove the seed. Place four pieces in the center of each plate and cover with lime juice, then salt and pepper to taste.

3. Turn the broiler on to "HI". Remove the tortilla pieces from the rack and place on the sheet pan, then cover each piece with refried beans, followed by the chorizo, jalapeno, and the three cheeses, then place under the broiler for about 90 seconds until the cheese melts. Place them on the plates around the avocado and garnish with cilantro.

The All-Day BLT

One sandwich we really enjoy is a bacon lettuce and tomato, or BLT, it's a real diner classic- not too filling and has lots of flavor. Over time our recipe has been updated to include homemade chipotle mayonnaise, for some more kick, along with avocado and beet pickled eggs, for more "staying power".

Ingredients

- 4 pieces thick cut bacon cut in half for 8 pieces
- 1 avocado seeded, peeled, and sliced longways
- 1 medium jalapeno sliced
- 2 beet pickled eggs with pickled beets and onions
- 1 large tomato sliced and cored (if necessary)
- 3 leaves romaine lettuce cored and cut in half
- 1 lime halved
- 4 slices 21 grain bread (or similar)
- 2 tbsp homemade mayonnaise
- 2 tsp crushed chipotle with adobo sauce
- 2 tbsp butter

1. Cook the bacon until it's just crispy and remove from the pan and drain.
2. While the bacon is cooking melt the butter on a griddle and drop on the bread slices- turning a couple of times until both sides are nicely browned turn off the heat. Mix the chipotle and mayonnaise together in a small bowl and set aside. Squeeze the lime's juice over the avocado slices, then salt and pepper to taste.
3. Place two slices of bread on the plates, then lay on the avocado slices and "smush" down with a fork, followed by the jalapeno slices. Next cover with the Romaine leaves torn or cut to fit, lay on the tomatoes as level as possible, then add the bacon across the top.
4. Cover the upper bread slices on the inside with chipotle mayonnaise and place them on top, pressing down to keep everything together, cut in half and plate, garnish with pickled eggs, beets, and onions.
5. Our beet pickled egg recipe and mayonnaise recipe are both in the "Basics" section.

Cast Iron Stir Fry

We've been trying new recipes for what I would call "take out", particularly Asian style dishes, since there aren't many around here. One we tried was a classic "Beef and Broccoli", which provided the inspiration for this dish, which allows us to use all the partial vegetables in the refrigerator, and just about any fresh or leftover protein. Break out the chopsticks!

Ingredients

- 2 tbsp brown sugar
- 2 tbsp minced garlic
- 1 tbsp minced ginger
- 1 tsp gochujang
- 1 tsp mirin
- ½ tsp sesame oil
- 1 tbsp cornstarch
- 2 tbsp soy sauce
- 2 tbsp oyster sauce
- ½ cup water
- 8-12 oz petite sirloin or ribeye (or pork shoulder, thin chops)
- 2 cups cooked jasmine rice
- ½ red pepper chopped
- 2 stalks celery split and chopped
- 1 large shallot sliced and chopped
- ½ medium onion sliced longways
- 4 oz mushrooms chopped (optional)
- 1-2 carrots peeled and chopped
- 2 cups broccoli florets
- 8 oz water chestnuts chopped
- ¼-½ cup vegetable stock
- 2 tbsp roasted peanuts
- 1 jalapeno cored and chopped
- 4 tbsp peanut oil for cooking

1. Thinly slice the meat then cut into 1-inch pieces, salt and pepper to taste. Mix the soy sauce, brown sugar, cornstarch, mirin, oyster sauce, sesame oil, water, garlic, gochujang, and ginger together in a bowl.

2. Heat 2 tbsp peanut oil to 350 °F in a large cast iron pan, drop in the meat and cook the first side for about 2 minutes, then flip them over for another couple minutes, until all the exterior red is gone, remove from the pan.

3. Drop two more tablespoons of peanut oil in and add the celery, carrot, onion, red pepper, mushrooms, shallots, and jalapeno to the pan, cook for about 3 minutes, then add the broccoli florets and stock. Cover the pan and cook for another 5-6 minutes, mixing and turning everything a couple times.

4. Remove the lid, the broccoli should have lightened in color, then pour in the sauce and mix well— cook for only a couple minutes, then drop the meat back in ,mix to coat everything, turn off the heat.

5. Lay the rice out on the plates then spoon the pan mixture over the top. Garnish with the chopped peanuts.

Pork Medallions and Plums

A few years ago we planted several plum trees out front, when the harvest comes in most of them end up on the grill. Carolyn turns pork tenderloin into these medallions, which are accompanied by a fresh spicy plum sauce. Our go-to side for this is Mrs. Millers Old Fashioned All Natural Egg Noodles.

Ingredients

- 1 lb pork tenderloin (a little more is ok)
- 2 eggs beaten
- 1 tsp fresh rosemary, finely chopped
- 1 tsp fresh sage, finely chopped
- 2 tbsp cornmeal
- 2 tbsp regular breadcrumbs
- 2 tbsp Panko
- 2 tbsp flour
- ½ tsp salt
- ½ tsp pepper
- Oil for frying (I use peanut oil)
- ½ bag (8 oz) cooked egg noodles
- 3-4 plums grilled, peeled, and sliced
- 2 tbsp honey
- 1 jalapeno cored and chopped
- 2 tbsp marsala wine
- 2 tbsp butter
- 1 shallot finely sliced
- 1 tbsp avocado oil
- ½ cup vegetable stock

1. Slice pork tenderloin into 1/4" slices, then use a mallet to make them even and wider.
2. In a saucepan combine the shallot, oil, and jalapeno and sweat for a couple minutes, then drop in the plums and marsala allow to cook off for a few minutes. Next add the honey and stock, stir, bring to boil, then simmer and reduce by 25% till thickened. Add the butter near the end, then salt and pepper to taste. Remove from the heat.
3. Heat the oil in a deep cast iron pan to 375 °F and check often while cooking.
4. In a large deep bowl, add the rosemary, sage, cornmeal, breadcrumbs, panko, flour, salt, and pepper and whisk together.
5. Dip the pork slices into the bread crumb mixture, then into the eggs and then back into the bread crumb bowl shaking off the excess.
6. Gently put the pork slices into the oil and monitor the bottom for browning (about 2 minutes or sooner) then turn each piece over and cook until that side is browned (about 2 minutes). Cook in batches to a temperature of 145 F for medium rare or 160 °F for medium.
7. Remove from the pan and place on a wire rack, then plate on the noodles and spoon on the sauce.

Port Braised Beef Shanks

There are certain cuts of meat I always pick up when they are available, like beef shanks, which are relatively inexpensive and very tasty. The first time I had these was in a Baltimore hotel during merger discussions in 2012 and I've enjoyed them since. This dish is inspired from New Scandinavian cooking's Braised Lamb Shanks" by Andreas Viestad, and is excellent as leftovers.

1. Heat the oil in a Dutch oven, add onions, carrots, mushrooms, and rosemary, sweat for a few minutes. Add the port wine, and cook for about 2 minutes. Preheat oven to 325°F.

2. Add the stock, shanks, salt, pepper, bay leaves, pepper flakes, and garlic; bring to a boil. Cover, then bake 90-120 minutes, stirring every 30 minutes.

3. Remove the shanks, and let rest. Add the dried mushrooms to the Dutch oven, then reduce the broth until brown and thick. Stir in butter, adjust salt and pepper at the end.

4. Debone the shanks, then slice into 3/8"-1/2" thick pieces, serve over mashed root vegetables, potatoes, or rice. Spoon gravy over the top, sprinkle with grated horseradish.

Ingredients

- 2 lbs beef shanks
- 2 cups vegetable stock
- ½ cup port wine
- 1 red onion sliced
- 1 carrot peeled and chopped
- 2 bay leaves
- 4 oz mushrooms
- 2 cloves garlic chopped
- 2 rosemary sprigs
- ½ tsp red pepper flakes
- 1 tsp salt
- 1 tsp pepper
- 2 tbsp fresh grated horseradish
- Handful dried chanterelle mushrooms (optional)
- 1 tbsp peanut oil
- 1 tbsp butter

Creamed Chipped Beef (SOS)

"SOS" or "Creamed Chipped Beef" was originally brought to the U.S. by Marines coming back from WW1 France and has been a staple of military cuisine for years. We used to get this fresh at small shops on the avenue, now we can only get the type that comes in a bag (Knauss), and bring it home from every trip out East. Recently we started using both bread and diner potatoes, or our fall back jalapeno biscuits.

Ingredients

- 3 homemade jalapeno biscuits or 4 slices 21 grain bread and home fries
- 3-4 oz dried/chipped beef cut into ½" pieces
- 2 ¼ cup milk
- 3 tbsp butter
- 3 tbsp AP Flour
- 1 tsp Tabasco Chipotle hot sauce plus finishing drizzle
- ¼ tsp Worcestershire sauce

1. Cut each biscuit in half then place on a heated griddle or pan and brown them, also heat up the other side when browned. Place browned side up on two plates. Toasted bread, or leftover mashed potatoes, or home fries can be used in place of biscuits.
2. In a large skillet, melt butter on medium heat, then add the dried beef and cook for one minute.
3. Add flour and stir for one minute to make a roux.
4. Slowly stir in the milk, teaspoon hot sauce and Worcestershire sauce, then raise the heat to medium-high.
5. Continue to cook while stirring often for about 6-8 minutes until the sauce is bubbling and thickens. Remove the heat before it seems done as it will continue to thicken as it cools. Add salt or pepper to taste.
6. Pour the beef sauce onto the biscuits, then drizzle on some hot sauce if desired and it's done.

Emeril's jalapeno biscuits are found on page 51 of "Essential Emeril", which we have modified to include:

- 1 tsp of brown sugar
- More buttermilk
- Cook at 425 °F rather than 375 °F

BJ's Capri Salad

I've always been a fan of the "Caprese" or "Capri" salad, that has been eaten for ages, primarily because we love tomatoes, mozzarella, and fresh basil. After I started making my own, it seemed like there was room for some heat in this classic, so I added jalapenos, white balsamic and stick pepperoni slices, complimented with grilled sourdough or Italian bread on the side, so it's a full meal.

Ingredients

- 2-3 Roma tomatoes sliced cored and cut in half
- 5 oz sliced mozzarella cheese
- 1 medium jalapeno cut in half, sliced, and cored
- 2 tbsp olive oil
- 2 tbsp white Balsamic vinegar
- 2 slices sourdough or Italian bread (I use Italian rolls split most of the time)
- 2 inches stick pepperoni
- 1 tbsp butter
- 1 Handful Fresh Basil
- Salt and pepper to taste
- Makes 2 Servings

1. Cut the mozzarella slices pieces in half, then arrange the cheese, and tomatoes alternately on each plate. Next lay jalapeno slices over the tomatoes. Drizzle the olive oil over the tomato/cheese and then the vinegar. Sprinkle with salt and pepper to taste, then drop on the basil (whole or torn).

2. Drop the tablespoon of butter (sourdough) or olive oil (Italian bread) on a griddle or large pan, allow to heat for a minute, then lay on the bread slices. Leave for about three minutes, then turn and heat for another three minutes (or until it starts to brown). Remove from the pan and place on the plate.

3. Slice the pepperoni into $1/8^{th}$ inch pieces and layer on the opposite side of the plate from the bread.

4. We'll make this for breakfast when we don't have a lot of time.

Pickled Grilled Cheese

When I was a kid, my grandmother would make grilled cheese for lunch a lot, with giant chunks of butter on the outside of the bread, browned in a pan, and they were great. Over the years I've experimented with many ingredients like sliced ham, or tomato, and finally landed on Famous Dave's spicy pickle chips, which give the sandwich a nice "pop". I always use both cheddar and pepper jack cheese, and cover the pan to keep the heat in to melt the cheese.

Ingredients

- 4 slices 21 grain bread or similar
- 2 oz medium cheddar cheese sliced off the block
- 2 oz pepperjack cheese sliced off the block
- 2 tbsp Dijon mustard
- 4-5 spicy pickle chips or 2 spicy spears chopped
- 1-2 tbsp butter

1. Lay out the first two pieces of bread, and spread on half the mustard, next sprinkle on the chopped pickles, then lay the slices of cheese alternately across the bread (should take 6-8 slices to cover the whole piece) and press them down to "anchor" the pickles. Spread mustard on the other slices of bread and place them on top.

2. In a large wide pan or griddle, melt the butter and spread around the pan, then place the sandwiches in and cover. Keep the heat around medium low and cook the first side for 3-4 minutes, press them down with a spatula, then carefully, flip over supporting the top, cover and cook another 5-6 minutes- checking the bottom a couple times- until nicely browned and the cheese looks melted. I normally try and flip onto an area that still has butter on it to minimize adding any more butter. Sometimes I'll flip twice depending on how the heat was working.

3. Remove from the pan, plate, salt, and pepper to taste, then cut in half and serve!

LO Rib and Pineapple Fajitas

Whenever we make ribs on the grill, along with pineapple or other fruits, there's always a couple ribs and fruit left over. My favorite way to repurpose them is in a fajita, with fresh vegetables cooked for short duration to maintain their crisp texture, chipotle sour cream instead of cheese, and sweet grilled pineapple to add depth. This is one dish we usually have in the morning since it's really easy and tastes great!

Ingredients

- 1 medium onion course chopped
- 1 large jalapeno course chopped
- 1 medium red bell pepper course chopped
- 1 avocado quartered
- ⅔ -1 cup cored chopped tomatoes
- 1 tbsp red wine vinegar
- Juice of 1 lime
- 2 heaping tbsp or 4 measured tbsp sour cream
- 1-2 tsp chopped chipotle w/adobo sauce
- 2 large (8-10 inch) tortillas
- 2 left over grilled ribs chopped
- Left over grilled pineapple
- Johnson's barbeque sauce

1. Heat up a flat cast iron pan and cook the tortillas, turning often, till they harden up. Place on each plate. Start heating up another cast iron pan. Sprinkle the red wine vinegar over the chopped tomatoes and set aside.

2. Mix the sour cream, chipotle, and one-half lime juice then set aside. Slice the avocado long ways into four pieces, place two on each plate and cut into smaller pieces. Squeeze one half of the limes juice over and salt and pepper.

3. Once the second cast iron pan reaches about 300 F throw in the onions and peppers. Stir often until the peppers change color and onions start to soften.

4. Place the leftover pineapple in the pan and continue to stir until the pineapple caramelizes some, then drop in the ribs. Cook for just a couple minutes, add more barbeque sauce if desired, then distribute to the tortillas.

5. Spoon the sour cream sauce on each tortilla, then cover with the chopped tomatoes. Done.

Saddle Butte Perogies

I always have a couple boxes of perogies in the freezer, for those times that we want something quick and easy that can utilize local fresh ingredients, and fits into any mealtime of the day. This dish, named after the hills we see out front, uses Spanish chorizo and chipotle sour cream to incorporate Southwest flavors into this classic.

Ingredients

- 12 frozen perogies (1 box)
- 1 ear left over roasted corn kernels removed (canned can be substituted)
- 1 medium avocado sliced and chopped
- 1 large or 2 Roma tomatoes cored and chopped
- 1 large jalapeno cored and chopped
- ½ red or orange pepper sliced and chopped
- 1 large shallot chopped
- 1 lime juiced
- 3 tbsp sour cream
- 1-2 tsp chipotle crushed with adobo sauce
- 12 pieces (approx. 1.5 oz) Spanish chorizo slices cut into 4's
- 2 tbsp avocado oil
- Cilantro for garnish

1. Cover the avocado with lime juice and combine in a large bowl with the corn, tomato, jalapeno, red or orange pepper, and avocado oil, salt and pepper to taste, then set aside.

2. In a large pan on medium heat place the Spanish chorizo in and allow to release its juices about 3 minutes, then drop in the shallots, stir around, next lay in the perogies and place the cover on. Check the pan every few minutes and turn the perogies, remove the cover and continue until they are browned on both sides. Add avocado oil if necessary.

3. While the perogies are cooking combine the sour cream and chipotle in a bowl then spread on the plates in a thin layer (where the perogies will sit).

4. Once the perogies are done, remove from the pan and position six around each plate in a circular pattern on top of the sour cream mixture, then spoon the avocado corn salsa around the top, place the pieces of crispy chorizo in the center and garnish with cilantro.

South Street Perogies

Years ago I worked as a meter reader in South Philly, and spent a lot of time on South street, even living at 24th and Lombard for a while. The inspiration for this dish comes from the multi national food found down on South street, and uses South Philly steak sandwich style toppings, pancetta for background flavor and texture, along with this central European classic perogies.

Ingredients

- 12 frozen perogies (1 box)
- ½ red pepper sliced coarsely chopped
- 1 large jalapeno cored, and coarsely chopped
- ½ onion sliced and coarsely chopped
- 2 handfuls of cherry tomatoes halved
- 2 tbsp red wine vinegar
- 3 tbsp sour cream 1-2 tsp chopped chipotles with adobo sauce
- 2 oz uncured pancetta chopped
- 1 large shallot chopped
- 2 tbsp olive oil
- Salt and pepper to taste

1. Dress the tomatoes with the red wine vinegar and set aside.

2. In a large pan on medium heat, place in the olive oil, and pancetta and allow to cook down about 3-4 minutes, then drop in the shallots, stir, next lay in the onions, and peppers , then the perogies and place the cover on. Check the pan every few minutes and turn or rearrange the perogies for even thaw and browning. Once they start to brown remove the cover and continue to cook until the onions are opaque and the perogies are browned on both sides (I usually mix everything up once the vegetables start to cook down).

3. While the perogies are cooking combine the sour cream and chipotle in a bowl then spread on the plates in a thin layer (where the perogies will sit).

4. Once the perogies are done, remove from the pan and position six around each plate in a circular pattern on top of the sour cream mixture, then spoon the vegetables around the top, followed by the cherry tomatoes, then salt and pepper to taste and serve.

Leftover Steak Fajita

Being an opportunistic shopper, I normally look for sales on steak around holidays to get a great deal for a large quantity. Grilled ribeye steaks are our favorite, and there is always leftovers after dinner, which work perfectly for fajitas. The smokey flavor of the meat, combined with seared and fresh vegetables, makes for a quick and awesome breakfast to start the day, or an easy dinner.

Ingredients

- 8 oz leftover grilled steak
- 1 medium onion course chopped
- 1 large jalapeno course chopped
- 1 medium red bell pepper course chopped
- 1 avocado quartered
- ⅔-1 cup chopped tomatoes
- 1 tbsp white balsamic vinegar
- Juice of 1 lime
- 2 heaping tbsp or 4 measured tbsp. sour cream
- 1-2 tsp chopped chipotle with adobo sauce
- 2 tbsp barbeque sauce
- 2 tbsp Cotija cheese crumbled
- 2 large or 4 medium tortillas
- Salt and pepper to taste
- Cilantro for garnish

1. Heat up a flat cast iron pan and cook the tortillas, turning often, till they harden up. Place on each plate. Start heating up another cast iron pan (I use a flat iron pan for my tortillas). Sprinkle the balsamic vinegar over the chopped tomatoes and set aside.

2. Mix the sour cream, chipotle, and a squirt of lime juice then set aside. Cut the steak into 1/2" to 3/4" pieces.

3. Slice the avocado long ways into four pieces, place two on each plate and cut into smaller pieces. Squeeze one half of a lime's juice over and salt and pepper to taste.

4. Once the cast iron pan reaches about 325 F throw in the onions, red pepper, and jalapeno. Stir often until the peppers change color and onions start to soften.

5. Move the vegetables to the outside of the pan and drop in the steak pieces, while keeping the pan hot. Cook for just a couple minutes to heat them up, mix together and stir in the barbeque sauce, then place on the tortillas.

6. Spoon the chipotle/lime sauce on each tortilla, cover with the chopped tomatoes, then sprinkle on the cotija cheese and its done. Garnish with fresh cilantro and add a piece of lime to each plate if desired.

Hilltop Haluski

I recently found a recipe for Alexander Bodnar's "Pittsburgh Haluski", and since we really like cabbage dishes, I had to try it. I enjoyed the Eastern European flavors (including our favorite PA Dutch egg noodles) and then adapted this to fit more with our Southern and New Scandinavian cooking points of view, it's a new favorite!

Ingredients

- 2-4 links andouille sausage
- ½ head green cabbage cored and sliced thin
- 2 medium apples peeled, cored, and sliced
- 1 large or 2 medium onions halved and sliced thin
- 1 large jalapeno cored and sliced
- 2 tsp Dijon mustard
- 3 cloves garlic
- 2 tbsp butter
- 8-12 ounces PA Dutch egg noodles (or personal preference)
- 1 tbsp fresh dill chopped
- 1 tbsp apple cider vinegar
- 4 oz noodle water
- 3 tbsp peanut oil

1. Add 2 tbsp butter and 2 tbsp peanut oil to a wide nonstick pan, at medium heat, then add the jalapenos, cabbage, and onions, cover and cook for about 10 minutes, stirring often, until the cabbage is reduced in size.

2. Cook the PA Dutch egg noodles per instructions, drain and set aside, keep about ½ cup of the water for the final dish.

3. While the cabbage is cooking, heat 1 tbsp of peanut oil in a cast iron pan, add in the andouille and cover, at medium low heat for about 8 minutes, turning every two minutes until browned. Remove from the pan, rest for 5 minutes, then cut into 3/8" pieces.

4. Once the cabbage is reduced add the garlic, apples, Dijon, cider vinegar, and half the noodle water, mix to combine, cook another 4-6 minutes stirring often. Next add the noodles and remaining noodle water, dill, then salt and pepper.

5. Plate the cabbage, noodles, onions, and apples, top with the sliced andouille and its done! Brussels and leftover ham can be substituted for the cabbage and andouille.

Potato and Chorizo Crispy Tacos

My friends and I had lunch recently at a small Mexican restaurant in Glendale Arizona, and we had potato tacos, which were like normal tacos but with a hard, crispy shell, so I had to try this at home. Since we already have a duck fat potato recipe I wanted to incorporate that and fresh chorizo, then make my own hard taco shells along with a chipotle, lime sour cream dressing. It's one of our new favorites now!

Ingredients

- 1.5 lbs Yukon Gold potatoes
- ½ medium red onion chopped fine
- ¼ red pepper chopped fine
- 1 jalapeno cored and chopped
- 4 flour tortillas (8 inch)
- 4 oz fresh chorizo
- 2 tbsp duck fat
- 2 tbsp sour cream
- ½ tsp crushed chipotles
- 2-3 tbsp lime juice
- 1 tbsp kosher salt
- Peanut oil for frying

1. Dissolve the salt in a medium bowl, then peel and chop the potatoes into 1/2 inch cubes, add to the bowl, mix and let sit for 15 minutes. Dry them well before cooking! In a small bowl combine the sour cream, lime juice, and chipotles and mix well to a thin sauce.

2. While the potatoes are soaking heat 1/2-inch oil in a medium cast-iron pan up to about 380 degrees (really watch the temperature). Pick up a tortilla in the middle with tongs, fry one half for 30-60 seconds, then turn over and fry the other side. Place on a taco rack.

3. Bring the duck fat up to about 375 °F in a wide nonstick pan, then lay in the potatoes. Allow the first side to brown then flip them over and cook about 4 minutes more- then add the vegetables, stir everything up, and cook a few more minutes- just till the onions soften.

4. While the potatoes are cooking drop the chorizo in a small pan and cook on medium low heat until it is rendered.

5. Once everything is done, place the tortillas on plates, spoon some chorizo into each tortilla followed by the potato mixture and finally drizzle the sauce over each.

Waffle House Tribute

No matter where I have traveled to in our Country, one thing that is always consistent-Waffle House- you always know what you are getting when you sit down at the counter. The way orders are taken and then "called" to the cook (who always gets it right) is amazing and the food is always delicious. In honor of all those experiences I've had there, I now make my own version of this Classic American breakfast!

Ingredients

- 2 medium Yukon gold potatoes peeled
- 1 small onion finely chopped
- 1 jalapeno finely chopped
- 5 eggs divided
- ⅓ -½ cup AP flour
- 3 tbsp duck fat
- ½ cup grits cooked per package (4 servings)
- 4 pieces pork roll, or 4 slices scrapple, or 6 pieces bacon
- 2 homemade biscuits
- 2 tbsp butter
- 2 tbsp apple butter
- Avocado oil spray
- Louisiana hot sauce
- Salt and pepper to taste

1. Grate the potatoes into a towel to dry them, then add to bowl along with the onion and jalapeno and mix together well. Add one beaten egg to the bowl along with 1/3 cup of flour, and 1 tsp salt. Mix everything together again- if it's too loose add more flour. Use a large slotted spoon to make the pancake size uniform while the duck fat heats.

2. Heat the duck fat in a cast iron pan heat to 350 °F and add the latkes carefully, let cook on one side till they start to brown, then turn over till the other side's brown- remove from pan to a rack and then to the plates.

3. Cut the two biscuits in half and place on grill or griddle until browned, then top both halves with apple butter and plate.

4. Cook the grits using package directions to get about 1 cup. The age-old struggle on how to dress grits is a deeply personal thing, I just use some butter and salt and pepper.

5. Heat avocado spray in a wide pan, crack and drop in the 4 eggs, allow to cook a few minutes, then cover until the top cooks, garnish with hot sauce and salt and pepper to taste.

6. Finally add your preferred breakfast meat and it's done!

On The Grill

Prospectors Burger

I've always enjoyed a hamburger right off the grill, and in the southwest we enjoy chorizo, so I combined the two, which gives the patties some authority and helps keep it moist. Instead of using store bought condiments, fresh quick pickled ingredients are used to brighten up the dish, and provide a "pop".

Ingredients

- 6 oz ground angus beef or bison
- 4 oz fresh chorizo
- ½ large red onion sliced thin and halved
- 1 large jalapeno sliced
- ⅓ cup apple cider vinegar
- ⅓ cup sugar
- ½ cup water
- Handful fresh spinach
- 2 tbsp grated fresh horseradish
- 2 large burger rolls (tailgaters or similar with sesame seeds)
- Peanut or avocado oil for grilling

1. Whisk the apple cider vinegar, sugar, and water together until the sugar dissolves, then add the sliced red onions and sliced jalapenos. Let stand for 30-60 minutes stirring several times.

2. Heat the grill up to medium high about 400 °F with a cast iron pan set on the grill. While the grill is heating combine beef/bison and chorizo very well and make two patties- season with salt and pepper.

3. Place the burgers and 1 tbsp oil in the cast iron pan, for between 8-10 minutes (for a medium burger) turning every couple minutes. While the burgers are cooking place the rolls on the grill until they get nice grill marks then pull everything off and allow the burgers to rest.

4. Finally, assemble each burger on the plate by placing fresh spinach on the bottom bun, lay on the patty, cover with the pickled onions and jalapenos, then top with fresh horseradish.

5. We normally make fried Brussel sprouts with these, in the "Sides" section, or French potato salad.

Ranchhand Thin Burgers

We blend bison or beef with chorizo for burgers, inspired by Adam Ragusa's "thin burgers" YouTube video. They're smaller, less heavy, and perfect for bulk prep. We make six burgers with six Taste of Home "Potato Rolls," then freeze them individually for quick grilling.

Ingredients

- 1 lb ground beef
- 8 oz fresh pork chorizo
- 4 oz butter
- 6 homemade burger buns (or artesian rolls)
- 1 large tomato sliced and cored
- 3-4 leaves romaine lettuce cored
- 4 oz pepper jack cheese/sharp cheddar sliced
- ½ medium red or white onion sliced thin
- 1 jalapeno sliced thin
- 1 avocado peeled, seeded and sliced longways
- 8-10 Famous Dave's pickle chips
- Juice of 1 lime
- 3-4 tbsp "Johnson's barbeque sauce" or similar.

Thin Burgers Process:

1. Place the butter in a small saucepan and heat until it melts, then simmer until it separates. Spoon off the top foam and allow to cool slightly.

2. In a large bowl, break up the beef and chorizo, then hand mix to combine thoroughly. Make 6 equal-sized balls, using a scale for accuracy.

3. Cut out 12 burger-sized pieces of waxed paper. Lay out 6 pieces, shiny side up.

4. Roll each meatball in the cooled butter, place on waxed paper, and gently smash down. Place another piece on top, shiny side down, and press until even. Repeat for the remaining 5 burgers.

5. Wrap two patties and two buns together in freezer wrap, place in a freezer bag, seal, and write the date on it. Repeat two more times.

6. The quantity of ingredients listed, besides the beef, chorizo, and buns, is for one set of burgers. Adjust as needed.

Steps Ranchhand Burger:

1. Pull one package of burgers and buns out and allow the buns to defrost on the counter (unwrapped) place the burgers in the refrigerator.
2. Preheat the grill to between 450- and 500° F.
3. Squeeze the lime juice on the avocado slices, then sprinkle with salt and pepper.
4. Once the grill hits temperature, place the buns on and allow to get nice grill marks on the insides, then turn over and heat the outside also, pull off the grill.
5. Pull the top piece of wax paper from each burger then lay on the grill using the remaining piece. Cook these for about 4-5 minutes on the first side, then flip over and cook another 3-4 minutes. Drop on the cheese, turn off the grill, and allow to heat another few minutes to melt the cheese, then remove from the grill.
6. Place the bun bottoms on plates, lay on the avocado pieces and "smush" them down, followed by the jalapenos, then lettuce, onions, tomatoes, burger, and then pickles. Spoon the barbeque sauce on the bun tops and place on top.
7. Normally we don't need a side with this, but grilled veggies or fruit work well.
- We use the TOH recipe for "Easy Potato Rolls" for our buns (along with sesame seeds)

"Easy Potato Rolls"

On The Grill 49

Brandy Marinated Grilled Pineapple

One of our favorite ways to enjoy fresh fruit like peaches, plums, pears, and pineapple is to grill them. There's nothing like adding that smokey char and flavor to really enhance the taste of many dishes. For pineapple, we've developed a marinate that supports its natural taste and adds some sweetness and depth, making it perfect with ribs and in rice.

Ingredients

- 1 pineapple remove top, bottom, skin, cored and sliced into rings
- 1 tbsp good quality brandy
- 2 tsp fermented pepper hot sauce (not vinegar based) or similar
- 1 tbsp dark brown sugar
- 2 tbsp peanut or avocado oil
- ¼ tsp salt
- ¼ tsp pepper

1. Using a large Ziplock bag, add all the ingredients except the pineapple and mix very well.

2. Add the pineapple to the marinate and mix well by kneading and turning over several times. Allow to rest 30-60 minutes turning a couple times.

3. Place the pineapple slices on the grate of a grill at around 400 °F for about 3 or 4 minutes, then turn over and cook for another 3-4 minutes or until it softens some. Pull from the grill and remove to a dish to serve.

4. These are great as leftovers, with rice dishes, and ribs, pork chops, or ham.

Carolyn's Grilled Corn

One of my favorite things to grill is fresh corn. It's really a great food right off the grill, but I use it most in its leftover form, always having several ears in the refrigerator. We include it in omelets with chorizo, ham bone chowder, rice, orzo, and many other dishes, and it's a relatively inexpensive way to stretch a food dollar when in season.

Ingredients

- 4 ears fresh corn
- 4 tbsp butter softened
- Salt and pepper

1. Set the gas grill to "high" and allow to heat up. Remove the husks from the corn (send the husks to the compost pile) and remove any silk.

2. Using a large plate rub each piece of corn with butter to coat, then salt and pepper the entire surface. Allow to rest for about 10 minutes.

3. Place the corn on the grill and cook at high for two minutes (with the top closed), then rotate 90 degrees every 2 minutes for a total of 8 minutes. Remove from the heat.

4. Additional spices can be sprinkled on prior to or after cooking, one of our favorites is to brush on chopped chipotle with adobo sauce right when its finished.

5. Normally we make this while ribs or other meats are cooking, along with any fruit that needs grilling. Adding some fruit wood chips to the grill will provide a nice smoky taste.

6. Leftover corn will last a week in the refrigerator if wrapped in plastic wrap or in a freezer bag.

Juniper Grilled Game Hens

For many years we would pick up game hens and then roast them, but they tended to dry out, so I started to look at a better method to keep them moist and add more flavor. After watching Andrias Viestad grilling all kinds of proteins, we started using our local juniper wood chips, and our homemade barbeque sauce, to add a nice smoky flavor to them. While they are cooking it's a great time to also grill some pineapple, corn, or zucchini for vegetable corn rice!

Ingredients

- 2 Game hens
- Juniper chips (or similar)
- "Johnson's Barbeque Sauce"
- Olive oil
- Salt and pepper
- 2 cups cooked rice
- Corn
- Pineapple
- Zucchini or other vegetables of choice

1. Unpackage the birds and allow them to thaw and warm near room temperature. Next turn them over and remove the backbones (spatchcock), then rinse and pat dry. Rub olive oil into the skin and sprinkle the inside and outside with salt and pepper.
2. Set the grill to "high" and allow to heat up to between 450- and 500-°F. Make sure the grates are clean and oiled.
3. Once the grill is hot place the birds on one side of the grill, inside down, and allow to roast for about 10 minutes, then flip and roast for another 10 minutes, add the juniper to the grill, flip and then roast another 10 minutes (the inside should be down).
4. Turn the heat off on the burner under the birds and add any vegetables to the other side of the grill while the hens are smoking. Baste with barbeque sauce and turn/baste about every 5 or so minutes for the next 20 -30 minutes, until the internal temperature is 165 F. Remove from the grill and allow to rest for 8 minutes before carving.
5. I normally cut the birds in half and plate one half over grilled vegetable corn rice (recipe in the "Sides" section); additional barbeque can be added on top if necessary.
6. The Johnson's Barbeque Sauce recipe is in the "Basics" section.
7. Any leftovers are great for a spicy chicken salad the next day.

Grilled Country Style Ribs and Pineapple

I grew up eating grilled "Country Style Ribs", although in those days my Father would boil them, then grill them to well done, which is not the way I like them! Now that we make our own barbeque sauce, with all fresh ingredients and some heat, I use that for basting. These are great with vegetable corn rice, and awesome as leftovers for breakfast fajitas.

Ingredients

- 2 lbs country style ribs
- 8 oz Johnson's barbeque sauce (or similar)
- Juniper wood chips (or similar)
- 1 Pineapple remove top, bottom, skin, cored and sliced into rings
- 1 tbsp good quality brandy
- 2 tsp Tabasco Chipotle hot sauce (or similar)
- 1 tbsp dark brown sugar
- 2 tbsp peanut or avocado oil
- ¼ tsp salt
- ¼ tsp pepper

1. Pull the ribs out of the refrigerator and allow them to warm up near room temperature.

2. Using a large Ziplock bag, add all the ingredients except the ribs, barbeque sauce, and pineapple then mix well. Add the pineapple to the marinate and mix by kneading and turning it over several times. Allow to rest 30-60 minutes turning a couple times.

3. Heat the grill to at least 400 °F, lay on some wood chips, then drop the ribs on and allow to sear for about two minutes per side (I start with the bone side for 3-4 minutes first) until all four sides show grill marks normally about 10 minutes.

4. Turn off the far-right burner (on a 3-burner gas grill) and move the ribs over to that side and allow to cook another 10 minutes or so, turning a couple times while the wood chips burn off. Next start applying the barbeque sauce with a long-handled brush after each turn for another 10 minutes. Once the sauce starts to dry up on the rib exterior, and the internal temperature is above 145F, they are done.

5. Near the end of cooking the ribs place the pineapple slices on the grill for about 3 or 4 minutes, then turn over and cook for another 3-4 minutes or until they soften. Pull from the grill, then pull the ribs, and remove to a dish to serve.

Grilled Ribeye Steak

The ribeye steak is by far our favorite cut of beef since it has so much flavor. It can be used for many types of dishes including, of course, steak sandwiches (a real favorite), but right off the grill with a baked potato is perfect! it's good for any time of the day, super easy to cook on the grill, and great as a leftover. Whenever they go on sale, I pick several packs up stock up the freezer for later.

Ingredients

- 1 lb ribeye bone in steak (approximate)
- ½ tsp cayenne pepper
- 1 tsp garlic powder
- 1 tsp onion powder
- 1 tsp chili powder
- 1 tsp smoked paprika powder
- ½ cup Johnson's barbeque sauce (or similar)

1. Pull the steak out of the refrigerator and allow it to warm up some. Mix the garlic, onion, cayenne, smoked paprika, and chili powder together and apply liberally to both sides of the meat and rub it in well, then allow to soak in for about 20 minutes. Place the Johnson's barbeque sauce (or personal favorite) in a small pan and heat at low until reduced about 50%. Remove from the heat and set aside.

2. While the rub is soaking into the steak heat the grill up to about 450 °F and clean the grates off. Drop the steak in the center of the grill and lower the lid, allow to cook for 2-3 minutes (based on the thickness of the steak), watch for the top side to get "wet", then flip over for another 2 minutes or so for rare towards medium, another minute for medium. Using tongs pick the steak up and hold the sides on the grill working around the outside, then pull from the heat and allow to rest on a plate or board for about 8 minutes. We like to have it what I call "rare towards medium", similar to how we cook tuna loin.

3. Slice off any large sections of fat around the exterior and remove the bone. Then slice the steak on a bias into about ½ inch slices. Lay the steak over whatever side is being used (like rice, mashed roots, orzo, etc.), salt and pepper to taste, then drizzle a line of barbeque sauce down the center of the steak slices.

Smoked Duck Breast with Cherry Port Sauce

Our favorite way to make duck breast is on the grill and smoked with some of our local juniper wood chips "Nordic style", then combined with a cherry port sauce that incorporates homemade duck stock, juniper berries from our trees, local honey, and a hot pepper for some heat. This combination of flavors is just awesome and goes with many sides, my favorite being duck fat potatoes.

Ingredients

- 2 duck breasts
- Juniper wood chips
- 2 tbsp of Avocado or Olive Oil divided
- 1 small shallot sliced
- 1 Serrano or Jalapeno pepper cored and chopped
- ¼ cup duck or vegetable stock
- ½ cup of Port wine (red wine can be used instead)
- 2 tbsp Balsamic vinegar
- 2 tbsp local honey
- 1 tbsp butter
- ¼ tsp about 5 ground Juniper berries
- 1 tbsp cherry preserves
- 8 oz of pitted cherries (fresh or frozen)

1. Heat 1 tbsp oil in a saucepan, add shallot and pepper and cook until they soften, about 2 minutes.

2. Add stock, wine, vinegar, honey, butter, Juniper berries, cherry preserves and pitted cherries to the pan, cook until the liquid is halved, and cherries are cooked down, about 20 minutes. Salt and pepper to taste.

3. While the sauce is cooking heat the grill (cast iron pan on the grate) to 450 °F along with a handful of juniper (or similar) wood chips on one side of the grate.

4. Score the skin/fat side of the duck breasts criss cross, careful to not hit the meat, salt and pepper both sides.

5. Place 1 tbsp oil in the heated pan, lay the breasts in skin side down, and cook until they brown and the fat renders (about 5-6 minutes). Move the pan away from the heat (turn off a burner for gas) and allow to heat through while the juniper is smoking for another 5-6 minutes (until the meat reaches 140 °F degrees for medium rare). Pull from the grill, allow to rest 8-10 minutes before cutting, then slice the breasts across the grain, lay on top of your preferred side, and spoon some sauce over each.

Barbeque Smoked Salmon

Salmon became a featured dish in our house after watching Andreas Viestad, of New Nordic Cooking, wrestle one from a river by hand, then cook several great dishes with it. Our local supermarket recently started carrying "sushi grade" salmon blocks, which are perfect for grilling.

Ingredients

- 2 pieces sushi grade salmon (8-10 ounces combined)
- 1 tbsp Kosher salt
- 1 tbsp organic raw cane sugar
- 2 cloves garlic finely chopped
- ½ jalapeno finely chopped
- 1 shallot finely chopped
- 1 tsp lemon juice
- 1 tsp local honey
- ¼ cup white wine
- ½ cup duck stock (or similar)
- 2 tbsp peanut or avocado oil divided
- 3 tbsp butter divided
- Parsley
- Juniper chips

1. Rinse off and pat dry the salmon pieces, sprinkle on all sides with the salt and sugar, then allow to rest and warm up while the grill is heating up.
2. For the sauce heat 1 tbsp oil in a medium saucepan, then add the shallots and jalapeno, and allow to sweat for about two minutes, then add the garlic and sweat an additional minute followed by the wine and allow to cook out a couple minutes. Next add the stock (duck is preferred but vegetable works fine), lemon juice, honey, mix well and allow to cook down by about 50%, then add the butter near the end. Remove from the heat.
3. Heat a cast iron pan, with 1 tbsp oil and 1 tbsp butter on the grill, to around 400 °F along with some juniper chips on the grate, so they start to burn. Once the chips start to smoke add the salmon to the pan and sear each side for about one minute, closing the lid after each turn, until it shows a nice crust all around. By this time the smoke should be strong, so watch your eyes! Turn off the heat and allow to "smoke" for another few minutes or so, to a temperature of 120-125 °F, then remove from the heat and rest.
4. Plate the salmon on whatever side you like (my personal favorite is vegetable orzo), then drizzle the sauce over both pieces of fish, and garnish with parsley.
5. This approach works with a normal filet as well, just cook skin side down for about three quarters of the time then flip over to finish.

Marinated Pork Chops with Plum Chutney

Here's a great way to elevate an affordable, frequently discounted cut of meat while incorporating grilled fresh fruit.

Ingredients

Pork:
- 2 bone-in pork chops (approx. 1 lb. total)
- 1 tsp cayenne pepper
- 1 tsp smoked paprika
- 1 tsp onion powder
- 1 tsp chili powder
- 2 tsp dark brown sugar
- 1 tbsp cider vinegar
- 1 tbsp avocado oil

Chutney:
- 3-4 plums pitted and sliced in half
- 2 tbsp honey
- 1 jalapeno cored and chopped
- ½ cup port
- 2 tbsp butter
- 1 tbsp avocado oil
- ½ cup vegetable stock
- Salt and pepper

1. Mix the cayenne, smoked paprika, onion powder, chili powder, brown sugar, oil, and cider vinegar together. Cover the chops on both sides with the mixture and allow to rest for at least 30 minutes.
2. While the pork is resting place the plums on the grill flesh side down, heated to around 400F, and allow to cook for about 5 minutes. Turn them over and cook for another few minutes then remove from the heat.
3. Drop the chops onto the grill still at 400 °F and allow to cook about 3 minutes (for ¾ inch thick) then turn over and cook the other side for another three minutes (to internal temperature above 145 °F). Remove it from the grill and make the sauce while they rest.
4. In a saucepan combine the shallot, oil, and jalapeno and sweat for a couple minutes, then drop the plums and port in, cook off for a few minutes. Next stir in honey and stock, bring to boil, then simmer and reduce by 25% till thickened, add butter near the end, salt, and pepper to taste.
5. Place the chops on top of whatever side is made (I like dirty rice with this) then spoon the chutney over everything and enjoy.

Hoagies and Sandwiches

Two Street Grinder

Growing up in Philadelphia the hoagie, like the cheesesteak, is part of the cultural fabric of the city. Its origin comes from a sandwich shipyard workers at Hog Island (on the Delaware River) would eat, originally called the "Hoggie" however the Philly accent transformed it to "Hoagie" over the years. I always asked for my hoagie toasted, which was called a grinder. I make these using Amoroso rolls shipped in fresh from the East Coast which gives the sandwich that original "Philly" taste.

Ingredients

- 2 medium Italian rolls
- 2 tbsp Boars Head Deli Dressing
- 2 tbsp Cento Cherry Pepper Hoagie Spread
- 6 slices provolone
- 8 slices pepperoni
- 6-8 slices hot capicola
- 4 slices black forest ham or similar
- ¼ cup finely chopped onions
- 2-3 Romaine lettuce leaves cored and chopped
- 2 Roma tomatoes cored and chopped (and or
- cherry tomatoes)
- 1-2 tbsp red wine vinegar
- Salt and pepper

1. Slice the rolls and gently roll them over to not break the "hinge", then place them on a baking sheet. Spread a line of Boars Head deli dressing on the thick half and spread the Cento cherry pepper spread on the thinner half. Turn on the oven to 350 °F.

2. Build each sandwich by first placing the provolone cheese on the bottom (to support the "hinge"), then place the pepperoni on one side of the roll, the capicola on the other, then the ham down the middle.

3. Soak the tomatoes in red wine vinegar for a few minutes on the cutting board. Sprinkle the chopped onions on both sandwiches, followed by the lettuce, and finally the tomatoes, then add salt and pepper.

4. Place the baking sheet in the oven for about 8 minutes, then pull them out to plate, cut in half and serve.

Delaware and Oregon Special
Pork Roll, Egg, and Cheese

My appreciation for breakfast sandwiches on Italian rolls developed while working in generation station maintenance in Philadelphia. This sandwich is inspired by "Frank's", located west of the Delaware River on Oregon Avenue, which pumped these out all morning (like 6am) for everyone working along the river.

Ingredients

- 6-8 oz pork roll cut into 4 even slices
- 2 Italian rolls split
- 2.5-3 oz grated Asiago cheese
- 3 eggs
- ¼ cup half and half
- 1 tbsp olive oil
- Spray olive oil
- 2 cherry peppers cored chopped
- 3 tbsp Johnson's barbeque sauce (or personal choice)

1. Notch three sides of the pork roll (so it doesn't curl in the pan) and cook in a non-stick pan sprayed with olive oil over medium low heat, turning often, until browned. Remove from the pan and drain on paper towel then cut each piece in half.

2. While the pork roll is cooking, split the two rolls longways being sure not to break the "hinge". Heat up a large pan or griddle, add the olive oil and lay in the rolls rotating a couple times (it's good to use some weight for consistent browning). Once browned remove and lay on plates.

3. Whisk the eggs together with half and half then pour into a wide preheated pan at medium low (I use the same pan that the rolls were browned in). Allow to cook until the top starts to dry up, add the cheese across the center from side to side, and once the edges just start to brown flip one side towards the center, then the other side toward the center. Turn off the heat.

4. Spoon the barbeques sauce on both sides of each roll, place 4 half pieces of pork roll on one side of the roll, then cut the omelet in half at the center and again longways (I just use my spatula in the pan). Place two sections of omelet on each roll, keeping the outside ends facing in. Salt and pepper to taste, add the cherry peppers, cut, and serve.

Schuylkill Station Special
Scrapple, Egg, and Cheese

This sandwich is inspired by a small shop on the ground floor of the Schuylkill generating station (which dated back to 1912) near 26th and Christian streets in Philadelphia.

Ingredients

- 8 oz scrapple cut into 4 even slices
- 2 Italian rolls split
- 1.5 oz cheddar cheese grated
- 1.5 oz pepper jack grated
- 3 eggs
- ¼ cup half and half
- 1 tbsp olive oil
- Spray olive oil
- 2 cherry peppers
- 3 tbsp Johnson's barbeque sauce (or personal choice)
- Salt and pepper

1. Start the scrapple in a medium low nonstick pan sprayed with olive oil and allow to stiffen up on the underside (about 10 minutes), then carefully turn over and allow the other side to brown (about 8 minutes) flattening the patties also. Normally I turn one two more times until browned, it's a slow process but worth the time spent. Remove from the pan and drain on paper towel.
2. While the scrapple is cooking, split the two rolls longways being sure not to break the "hinge". Heat up a large pan or griddle, add the olive oil and lay in the rolls rotating a couple times. Once browned remove and lay on plates.
3. Whisk the eggs together with half and half then pour into a wide preheated pan at medium low (I use the same pan that the rolls were browned in). Allow to cook until the top starts to dry up, add the cheeses across the center, and once the edges just start to brown flip one side towards the center, then the other side toward the center. Turn off the heat.
4. Spoon the barbeque sauce on both sides of each roll, place 2 pieces of scrapple on one side, then cut the omelet in half at the center and again longways (I just use my spatula in the pan). Place two sections of omelet on each roll, keeping the ends facing inside. Salt and pepper to taste, add the cherry peppers, cut, and serve.

Roast Beef and Fried Onion Hoagie

The other day I was looking to finish off some roast beef lunchmeat, and I decided to try something different-including friend onions on the sandwich, and it turned out great, kind of like a "faux" steak sandwich in minutes. It's a quick and tasty meal that includes baby Swiss cheese, Amoroso Italian rolls, and our homemade "Revamped Russian Dressing".

Ingredients

- 2 Italian Rolls (like Amoroso)
- ½ lb. London Broil roast beef
- 6 slices baby Swiss cheese
- ½ medium sweet onion (5-6 oz) sliced longways
- 2-3 large romaine leaves cored and chopped
- ¼ cup "Revamped Russian" dressing (in "Condiment" section)
- 4 tbsp olive oil

1. Split the two rolls longways being sure not to break the "hinge". Heat up a large pan or griddle, add 1-2 tbsp olive oil and lay in the rolls rotating a couple times (its good to use some weight for consistent browning). Once browned remove and lay on plates and lay on the Swiss cheese so it can melt some.
2. In the same pan add the remaining olive oil, and once hot drop in the onions, cook for several minutes until they just start to caramelize, then remove from the pan with tongs and add to each sandwich.
3. Next place the roast beef onto each sandwich, followed by the Russian Dressing, and finally the lettuce, then cut in half and serve.
4. "Revamped Russian Dressing" is in the "Basics" section.
5. Left over roast beef sliced thin could be used for this recipe, if it's not overcooked, mushrooms and or hot cherry peppers will work also.
6. To make multiple sandwiches just increase the required quantities.

Garlic Chicken Cheese Steak

When Carolyn and I were living in a small apartment in Exton, PA. we dined at several really nice restaurants in the area often. We would take my kids out to an Italian restaurant on route 30 called "Rino's", lots of classics and great wings, but our favorite meal was their Chicken Cheesesteak, which was served on a garlic infused roll, and is the inspiration for this dish.

Ingredients

- 2 Amoroso (Italian hoagie roll) rolls split partly through
- 3 medium cloves garlic peeled and chopped finely
- 1 left over chicken breast (medium) sliced long ways, chopped in half
- 3 tbsp olive oil divided
- ½ large red pepper cored and sliced
- ½ large yellow onion sliced
- 2 large handfuls of spinach
- 6-8 medium to large mushrooms chopped
- 4-6 slices provolone cheese
- 3 tbsp "Franks" hot sauce
- 5 tbsp favorite BBQ sauce
- 1 tbsp butter melted

1. Heat one tablespoon olive oil in a large nonstick pan or griddle, drop in garlic and spread around, open the rolls, and lay in, then rotate at least once (an iron press helps here)- turn them upside down for a minute to heat the exterior. Once browned pull from the pan, plate and lay two or three slices of provolone on each roll.
2. In a well heated cast iron pan drop in the remaining two tablespoons olive oil, red pepper, onions, mushrooms, and allow to cook for a few minutes, then drop in handful of spinach and cover for about 2 minutes. Remove cover and allow to cook until the spinach is just wilted. Remove from the pan and spread evenly on both sandwiches.
3. Add more oil to the pan, if necessary, then heat it up to approximately 350F. Drop in the chicken, allow it to cook for a couple minutes and keep it moving around until it browns up.
4. While the chicken is cooking combine three tbsp of Franks hot sauce, five tablespoons of favorite BBQ sauce (I use Johnson's hot sauce), and one tablespoon of butter-stir into the chicken until well coated, then remove from the pan and evenly distribute on each sandwich. Cut each sandwich in half to serve.

Duke's Meatball Sandwich

One great way to use up leftover meatballs and sauce from a pasta dinner is to make meatball sandwiches, on a grilled Italian roll. One of the guys I worked with in the "High Volt Gang", who we called "The Duke" from his Vietnam era Marine Corps days, loved a good meatball sandwich, so this sandwich is named in his honor. This is definitely a Philly favorite and since our ground sausage has a lot of spice, hot peppers are optional, but provolone and basil are a must!

Ingredients

- 2 long Italian rolls
- 3 -4 leftover meatballs in red sauce
- 2 tbsp olive oil
- 4-6 slices provolone cheese
- 2 cherry peppers cored and chopped (optional)
- 1 tbsp grated Parmesan cheese
- 1 tbsp grated Romano cheese
- Fresh Basil leaves for garnish

1. Slice the Italian rolls and brown on griddle or large pan coated with the olive oil. Once browned turn over and allow outside to heat. Remove and plate, then add the provolone equally to each roll.

2. Cut each meat ball into a few pieces and add along with any leftover sauce to a deep pan, allow to heat slowly covered, until warmed through (I use a small Dutch oven).

3. Pile the meatballs along with some sauce on each sandwich, sprinkle with Parmesan, Romano, and basil, cut in half and serve- include a cherry pepper on the side for that South Philly feel.

Hot Roast Beef and Mozzarella Hoagie

After watching an episode of "Food Insider" that showcased a deli near Manhattan that makes their own mozzarella, and roast beef, into a great sandwich that people line up for, I made the same sandwich, which was awesome, but took a ton of time. This hoagie replicates that, but in much less time, since the "gravy" is made without the roast and is a cool use for deli roast beef!

Ingredients

- 1 large shallot peeled and sliced
- 1 large carrot sliced and chopped
- 2 celery stalks sliced and chopped
- ½ medium onion chopped
- 4 oz mushrooms sliced and chopped
- 1 Bay leaf
- 6-8 oz mozzarella sliced
- 2 cloves garlic peeled and minced
- ½ lb roast beef (London broil) or leftovers
- 32 oz beef stock
- 2 tbsp marsala wine
- 2 tbsp butter
- 1 tsp Worcestershire sauce
- 2 Italian long rolls
- ½ tsp pepper flakes
- Salt and pepper
- 5 tbsp olive oil
- Hot cherry peppers (optional)

1. In a Dutch oven combine the shallot, mushrooms, celery, carrots, onion, and three tbsp olive oil, then cook on medium high heat for 5-6 minutes.

2. Next pour in the marsala, and cook-off for about 1 minute, then add the Worcestershire, pepper flakes, garlic, butter, broth and bring to a boil. Reduce the heat and cook at low boil/simmer uncovered for about 20-25 minutes, until reduced about 25-30 percent. Salt and pepper to taste.

3. While the broth is cooking, in a large pan or griddle, drizzle in two tbsp of olive oil, place the rolls inside down (with a weight on top), then cook until browned, turning at least once. I normally flip them over at the end to heat the outside. Plate the rolls and lay the sliced mozzarella on both.

4. Once the broth has reduced, drop in the roast beef, mix well and allow to combine for about 1-2 minutes.

5. Pull the roast beef out of the pot and lay on the rolls, then spoon on as much gravy as you like (I make mine wet) add sliced hot cherry peppers, cut in half, and serve.

6. Save any leftover gravy, its excellent on mashed potatoes or Amish noodles.

Tailgate Tribute-Brats with Kraut

Beer brats are one of my favorite go to meals, especially the locally made Kiltlifter brats. I used to just throw them on the grill dry, until we watched a food blogger who taught the "German way", which uses a deep pan with about a third inch of very hot oil. I still use the grill and it works great with no clean up. We normally top them off with Edna's fermented cabbage kraut and a side of Catherine's baked beans.

Ingredients

- 2 Kiltlifter beer brats (or similar)
- 12 medium Italian rolls (Amoroso or similar)
- 4 pieces baby Swiss cheese
- 16 oz can baked beans
- ½ medium onion chopped
- 1 jalapeno cored and chopped
- 1 tsp molasses
- 2 tsp dark brown sugar
- 2 tsp apple cider vinegar
- 6-8 oz fermented cabbage Saur kraut
- 2 tbsp Dijon mustard
- 2 tbsp olive oil
- Peanut or avocado oil

1. Make the brats the German way- oil in cast iron or stainless pan at high heat (about 350 °F) using avocado or peanut oil, turning every two minutes for about 8 minutes until evenly browned, remove from the heat.

2. Split two Italian rolls (Amoroso or similar) and place on the grill until browned then place on plate, spread on the Dijon, then and add the Swiss cheese slices so they melt.

3. While the brats are cooking place the baked beans in a medium pot and stir in half of the onion and jalapeno along with the molasses, brown sugar, and apple cider, bring to a boil and then reduce to simmer till it melds and reduces a bit, about 6-8 minutes.

4. In an oiled skillet at medium heat, add the fermented cabbage (or Saur kraut), and the remaining chopped onions and jalapenos then cook down till the onions are opaque and cabbage has dried out some.

5. Place Saur kraut on top of the Swiss cheese on each roll, then add the brat on top. Use a slotted spoon to drain the beans off and add them to the plate and it's done.

Front Street Steak Sandwich

The cheese steak (invented in 1930) is a Philadelphia classic and I've eaten them all over the city. The key ingredients are shaved rib eye steak, fresh provolone cheese, fried onions and peppers, (or whatever vegetables you like), and of course hot cherry peppers. I don't use cheese wiz on my steaks, being influenced by many riverfront shops, like my favorite "Tony Luke's" down near Front and Oregon.

Ingredients

- 1 lb ribeye (approximate)
- 2 Amoroso or similar rolls
- ½ red pepper sliced and chopped
- ½ yellow onion sliced and chopped
- 4 oz mushrooms sliced
- 4-6 slices provolone
- 2 cloves garlic minced
- 1 shallot chopped
- 2 handfuls spinach
- 2 tbsp marsala wine divided
- 2 cherry peppers chopped and seeds removed
- 3 tbsp olive oil

1. Keep the meat very cold until just before slicing, then cut into 1/8" wide slices, then cut into pieces. Season with salt and pepper and set aside.

2. Slice the Italian rolls and brown on griddle or large pan coated with olive oil. Once browned turn over and allow outside to heat. Remove to plate, then add the provolone to each roll.

3. In a hot cast iron or similar pan add one tbsp olive oil then the mushrooms, onions, and red peppers. Cook until the pepper starts changing color and the mushrooms give up some liquid. Move the vegetables to the outside, drop in the meat allowing that to cook until it starts to brown, stirring often-don't overcook- keep the heat medium high. Mix everything together and then place on the rolls using tongs.

4. In the same pan drop a tbsp of olive oil and shallot, allow to sweat then add the marsala wine, spinach, and garlic, cover, and cook for about two minutes. Remove the cover and continue to cook for a couple minutes until the spinach starts to wilt and the wine cooks off. Using tongs cover each sandwich with the spinach mixture, then top with chopped cherry peppers. Cut in half and serve.

Phil's Pepperoni Pizza Steak

One of my early cooking experiences was making steak sandwiches with my best friend Phil, in his mother's rowhouse kitchen when we were about 12. Once the steak was done we dropped in some pepperoni and leftover pasta sauce, and created a perfect pizza steak. Phil has lived down Yuma way for almost 40 years now, and I finally made it to Arizona in 2008.

Ingredients

- 1 lb ribeye (approximate)
- 2 Amoroso or similar rolls
- ½ red pepper sliced and chopped
- ½ yellow onion sliced and chopped
- 4 oz mushrooms sliced
- 4-6 slices provolone
- 2 cloves garlic minced
- 1 shallot chopped
- 4 pieces deli pepperoni cut into quarters (or 10-12 slices stick pepperoni)
- 6-8 oz leftover pizza sauce (or pasta sauce)
- 2 cherry peppers, seeds removed and chopped
- 3 tbsp olive oil

1. Keep the meat very cold until just before slicing, then cut into 1/8" wide slices, then cut into pieces. Season with salt and pepper and set aside.

2. On a griddle or large pan heat 1 tbsp olive oil and drop in the chopped garlic. Lay the two rolls downside in the pan and use a weight, if possible, heat until browned. Once browned turn over to heat the outside. Remove to plates, then add the provolone equally to each roll.

3. In a hot cast iron pan add one tbsp olive oil then the shallot, mushrooms, onions, and red peppers. Cook until the pepper starts changing color and the mushrooms give up some liquid. Move the vegetables to the outside, drop in the last tbsp of olive oil and meat, allowing that to cook until it starts to brown. Stir often and do not overcook!

4. Next drop in the pepperoni and stir, then a minute later the tomato sauce and continue to cook until coated and reduced a bit (about 2 minutes). Remove from the heat. Using tongs remove from the pan and fill each roll. Garnish with cherry peppers, cut in half and serve.

5. Sliced deli pepperoni or stick pepperoni can be used, and mozzarella can be added if desired, we just like provolone by itself.

Left Over Barbeque Rib Sandwich

Whenever I see on sale spareribs they come home with me. I cook mine on the gas grill set at high, for about a one minute on each side, then shut the burner under the ribs off, adjust the temp to about 300 and let cook for 20 mins or so, turning and saucing often. Normally some fruits like pineapple or apples get grilled as well, and there are always leftovers, so we like to make leftover rib breakfast sandwiches!

Ingredients

- 2-3 ribs off the bone sliced and chopped
- 1 grilled apple sliced thin
- 1 tsp Dijon mustard
- 1 tsp chopped chipotle with adobo sauce
- 1 large shallot chopped
- 1 spring onion chopped (substitute another shallot if non on hand)
- 3 tbsp olive oil
- 2 tbsp marsala cooking wine
- ½ cup apple juice
- ½ tsp Johnson's BBQ sauce or similar)
- 2 Italian rolls
- 1 tbsp butter
- 1 handful spinach (optional)

1. Split the rolls partway through and "knead" them open so the hinge doesn't break. Heat a wide pan or griddle up, add 1 tsp olive oil, and place the rolls in. Using a weight helps get them evenly browned and turn a couple times. Pull from the pan when browned and place on the plates and top with the spinach.

2. Heat a cast iron pan to about medium along with 2 tbsp olive oil, then add the shallots and onions. Allow the onions to sweat then add the marsala, apple slices, spinach and cook for a couple minutes. Next add the mustard, chipotle, apple juice, BBQ sauce, butter and salt and pepper -allow to cook for a few more minutes (keep the heat up) then add pork and reduce the sauce until almost gone.

3. Spoon the mixture on the two rolls and pour over any remaining sauce. Breakfast is ready!

Seafood

Normandy

Baltimore Inner Harbor

First Mates Crab Stuffed Shrimp

The inspiration for this dish goes back to my youth, when we'd leave Philly for the Jersey Shore, to get a break from the heat. We would normally eat at one of the many seafood restaurants in town, where I'd see a half lobster stuffed with crabmeat ,and baked potato at every table. Instead of lobster I substitute butterfly shrimp and left-over root vegetable mash for the baked potato...I can still smell that salt air in my mind!

Ingredients

- 1 pound 16-20 count shrimp, peeled and deveined
- 8 oz crab claw meat chopped
- 10 crushed saltine crackers
- 1 egg
- 4 tbsp homemade mayonnaise divided
- 2 chopped green onions
- 2 tbsp grated fresh horseradish
- 1 tbsp Dijon mustard
- 1 tsp Worcestershire
- ¼ cup panko breadcrumbs
- ½ lemon
- Pinch cardamom
- Old Bay seasoning
- Leftover root vegetable mash
- 1 tbsp Parmesan
- 1 tbsp Romano
- 2 tbsp panko breadcrumbs

1. For the crab stuffing combine the saltines, 2 tbsp mayonnaise, green onions (white parts), one egg beaten, grated horseradish, Dijon mustard, Worcestershire sauce and crab meat in a large bowl and gently combine.
2. Split and butterfly the 16 shrimp and place in a lightly oiled glass baking dish. Add about one tablespoon of crab filling on top of each shrimp (even them out at the end) then lightly sprinkle with Old Bay. Place in the oven preheated to 350 °F for 30-35 minutes, broil for about 4 minutes at the end rotating the dish once.
3. In a lightly oiled baking dish, spoon in a layer of leftover root vegetable mash about 1 inch thick, then cover with Parmesan, Romano cheese and panko breadcrumbs. Place in the 350 °F heated oven for about 12 minutes, then broil for approximately 4-6 minutes, rotating the dish once (until browned). Allow to cool for several minutes then plate with the shrimp.
4. Whisk together two tbsp of homemade mayonnaise with juice of 1/2 lemon, pinch cardamom, salt, pepper, then spoon over the stuffed shrimp, garnish with green onions.

New Iberia Shrimp and Andouille

One of the things I remember from visiting our family down in Louisiana, as a kid, was the amazing number of gumbos and dishes that used andouille sausage and shrimp together. Once I was able to locate both items at my local market, I put together this dish that doesn't require a lot of time but has a depth of flavor, can use tomatoes from our garden, and utilize leftover vegetable corn rice.

Ingredients

- 1 lb shrimp (16-20s) cleaned and deveined
- 2 links andouille sausage casing removed and chopped
- 1 shallot
- 2-3 stalks celery chopped
- ½ onion chopped
- ½ red pepper chopped
- 2-3 Roma tomatoes chopped (or equal cherry tomatoes)
- 1 jalapeno chopped
- 3 cloves garlic
- 1 cup warm vegetable stock
- ¼ cup marsala wine
- 1 tbsp balsamic vinegar
- 2 tbsp butter
- 1 tsp brown sugar
- 1 tsp molasses
- 1 tsp Old Bay seasoning
- 2 tbsp peanut oil

1. In a large, preheated cast iron pan sweat the shallots in peanut oil, add the andouille and cook until it starts to brown up, then add the celery, onion, red pepper, and marsala. Cook for about 5 minutes at medium high heat.

2. Next add the vegetable stock, brown sugar, molasses, Old Bay, and tomatoes then bring back to a boil and cook to reduce by about one third.

3. While the andouille mixture reduces, heat another cast iron pan with the butter until over 350 °F, then drop the shrimp in and cook until the bottom starts to brown (about 2 minutes). Next add the garlic and turn over- cook another couple minutes until browned then add to the andouille mixture and mix thoroughly. Allow to reduce for a few minutes, mix in the balsamic and remove from heat.

4. I usually use about 2 cups of leftover vegetable corn rice (in the LOR Playbook "Sides" section) along with roasted okra, if available, to serve this on, but any rice would work. A nice piece of grilled cornbread or sourdough works well with this meal, and the shrimp shells can be used for stock.

Western Seared Scallops

There are a lot of great types of seafood out there, and one of our favorites is deep water scallops. Their size and rich texture really make an awesome meal, and I always combine some chorizo, and a few Southwest spices, to accent their natural flavor. Like most of our dishes from the sea its usually served on a bed of vegetable rice or vegetable orzo, simple and delicious.

Ingredients

- 16 oz scallops
- ½ tsp smoked paprika
- ½ tsp chili powder
- ½ tsp Old Bay
- ½ tsp garlic powder
- 2 tbsp butter
- 1 tbsp peanut oil
- 2 oz chorizo (or pancetta)

1. Drain and dry the scallops, then allow them to warm up for about 30 minutes before cooking.
2. Sprinkle the smoked paprika, chili powder, garlic powder, and Old Bay on one side of the scallops, covering their surface. I tend to use more chili powder but it's a personal preference.
3. In a cast iron or similar pan cook the chorizo (or pancetta) until it's starting to crisp up, then drop in the butter and the oil. Mix everything together and allow the pan to get to about 360 °F.
4. Drop the scallops in carefully (away from yourself) unseasoned side down. I usually adjust the heat up now to maintain the 360 or close to it. Cook the scallops for three minutes (move them around some to ensure they don't stick), then flip them over and cook for another two to three minutes. Remove any smaller ones first so they don't overcook.
5. Remove from the pan and plate, then pour the pan sauce and crunchy bits of chorizo (or pancetta) over top and enjoy!

Seafood

Xen Tuna Loin with Sushi Rice Blocks

When we lived near Bel Air Maryland we met and became friends with the sushi Master at Xen 16. He had worked many years and all over the world, so we would try all kinds of sauces and flavors with him. He worked long days starting at the docks before dawn, but always had time for us. I haven't mastered the art of sushi yet, but this dish is inspired by the things that Chef taught me.

Ingredients sushi rice sticks:

- 8 oz uncooked sushi rice
- 12 oz water
- 3 tbsp sake divided
- 2 tbsp jalapeno or Thai pepper cored and finely chopped
- 1 tsp toasted sesame seeds
- 2 tbsp ginger finely chopped
- 1 tsp mirin
- 1 tbsp rice vinegar
- ¼ cup plus 1 tbsp peanut oil

Ingredients tuna:

- .5-.75 lb. tuna loin
- 1 large avocado peeled and sliced
- Juice of 1 lime
- 3 tbsp "Magic Sauce" (in a squeeze bottle) or oyster sauce
- 1 tbsp peanut oil

Steps Xen Tuna Loin:

1. Make the rice per package directions, replacing 2 tbsp water with sake. Once it's done add the remaining ingredients except peanut oil and mix well.

2. Line a 9 X 9 or similar sized baking pan with wax paper then spoon in the rice mixture. Level it off with the spoon and press down with another pan until its compressed. Move to the freezer so that it firms up prior to cooking (at least 1 hour).

3. Drizzle lime juice on the slices of avocado, salt, and pepper to taste and set aside.

4. Once the rice is frozen, remove from the pan by turning upside down, cut the block in half , then cut "sticks or blocks" about ¾" wide. I usually freeze half since I'm only making two servings.

5. In a large cast iron skillet, drop in the ¼ cup peanut oil and bring up to about 375 °F. Drop the rice blocks in and cook on all sides, turning carefully- keep the heat at 375 °F!

6. Once the rice blocks are done move them to plates, drop the other tbsp of peanut oil into the pan, check the temp and drop in the tuna loin. Sear the first side about 90 seconds, turn over and sear the other side another 90 seconds. Then pick it up with tongs and run the sides of the loin on the pan and remove, allow to rest for about 5 minutes.

7. Drizzle the "Magic Sauce" (I use Helen Rennie's recipe) over the rice blocks slice the tuna on the bias and lay over the blocks, then lay the avocado on top. Garnish with sesame seeds.

Inner Harbor Crab Cakes

One of my favorite seafoods is blue claw crab, especially soft shells in the early summer, which we unfortunately can't get around here. While working and living near Baltimore I was able to develop an easy crabcake recipe inspired by Andrew Zimmern, and of course my favorite Inner Harbor restaurant "Miss Shirley's", down on Pratt Street.

Ingredients

Crabcakes

- 8 oz crab claw or lump meat chopped, drained and dried
- 10 crushed saltine crackers
- 1 extra-large or 2 small eggs beaten
- 2 tbsp homemade mayonnaise
- 2 chopped green onions
- ½ tsp Old Bay seasoning
- 2 tbsp grated fresh horseradish
- 1 tbsp Dijon mustard
- ¼ cup panko breadcrumbs
- ½ cup corn meal
- 1 tsp Worcestershire
- 1 tsp Louisiana hot sauce
- 2 tbsp unsalted butter
- 2 tbsp avocado or peanut oil

Sauce

- 2 tbsp homemade mayonnaise
- Juice of ½ lemon
- ½ tsp cardamom crushed
- Salt and pepper to taste

1. On a flat plate mix the corn meal, panko, and Old Bay.

2. Combine the saltines, white parts of the green onions, Old Bay, horseradish, Dijon mustard, Worcestershire, Louisiana hot sauce, mayonnaise, and the egg (s) in a large bowl, gently combine. Additional mayo may be required to get the right consistency. Separate the mixture into 4 "piles" (with large spoon) and roll into balls of equal size.

3. Roll the crab balls around in the corn meal panko mixture until well coated.

4. Heat the butter and oil in a large cast iron pan up to 350-375 °F, then place the balls in the pan and heat for a minute or so, then slowly press them out using a metal spatula. Cook on the first side for about 3 minutes (watching the heat), then when the bottom looks browned, gently flip over, heat the other side about 3 more minutes or until browned.

5. For the sauce, mix the homemade mayonnaise with the lemon juice and cardamom-add more lemon juice if too thick, then salt and pepper to taste.

6. I like to have these with corn fritters, or fried green tomatoes, and drizzle the sauce over both. Garnish with the green pieces of green onion.

Seared Garlic Shrimp Tacos

Our shrimp taco recipe has changed over the years from using store bought coleslaw mix in a bag, combined with a mayonnaise-based dressing, into an Asian inspired version using fresh cabbage, apple, and carrots. The shrimp are seared in cast iron with butter and garlic, and everything is topped off with a homemade mayo, cardamom, and lemon juice aioli, using eight-inch tortillas to hold it all together! I use any leftover slaw for pulled pork sandwiches.

Ingredients

- 1 lb of shrimp (21-25 count)
- 2 tbsp butter
- 2 cloves chopped garlic minced
- ½ head small green cabbage, thinly cut
- ½ head of small red cabbage, thinly cut
- 4 carrots, peeled and shredded or julienned
- 1 granny smith apple, peeled and cored, cut in matchsticks
- ½ jalapeno, cored and sliced
- 1 tbsp ginger, grated
- Juice from 1 clementine or orange, about 2 tbsp
- 4 tbsp rice vinegar
- 2 tsp Mirin
- 1 tsp Gochujang
- 1 tbsp peanut oil
- 5 drops of sesame oil
- ½ tsp sugar
- 1 tsp salt
- ¼ tsp white pepper
- 1 tsp sesame seeds (optional)
- ½ cup/handful of cilantro (optional)
- 4 large 8" tortillas
- 2 large tbsp homemade mayonnaise
- ½ tsp cardamom
- Lemon juice

1. Make the coleslaw dressing in a small bowl. Whisk together the orange juice, rice vinegar, mirin, Gochujang, peanut oil, sesame oil, sugar, salt, and pepper.
2. Combine the cabbage, carrots, apple, jalapeno, ginger, and sesame seeds, pour the coleslaw dressing on top and mix well. There will be plenty for leftovers.
3. Preheat a cast iron pan and heat each side of the tortillas until they stiffen up, a couple of minutes.
4. Defrost, peel, and rinse the shrimp, then them dry. The shells can be used for stock or go into the compost.
5. Preheat the cast iron pan to 375 – 400 °F. Add butter and heat until melted, then add the shrimp- keep the pan hot- and allow to cook for two minutes on the first side, flip the shrimp, add the garlic, and cook for another two minutes.
6. Combine homemade mayo, lemon juice, and cardamom, then set aside. Add more lemon juice if required to thin to a nice consistency. Salt and pepper to taste.
7. Place the tortillas on the plates, then add coleslaw, shrimp, and drizzle the sauce on top— garnish with cilantro.

Cast Iron Barbeque Shrimp

After searching for and finding an easy fried rice recipe, it was time to come up with something "shrimp" to go along and make a great dish. So, inspired by Rajat Parr's "Chile Shrimp", I included my homemade "Johnson's Barbeque Sauce" along with pepper flakes and peanut oil. It's a great way to use up that half bag of shrimp hanging around in the freezer!

Ingredients

- 1 lb 21-25 shrimp, peeled and patted dry
- 4 tbsp Johnson's Hot Sauce
- 4 tbsp vegetable stock
- 2 tbsp peanut oil
- 1 tbsp unsalted butter
- 2 tbsp lemon juice
- 2 tbsp soy sauce
- 2 scallions whites and greens separated
- 1 tbsp fresh ginger minced
- 1 large jalapeno cored and chopped
- 1 small lemongrass stalk white portion only finely chopped
- 2 cloves garlic finely chopped
- ½ tsp pepper flakes

1. Heat up a large cast iron skillet with 2 tbsp peanut oil and 1 tbsp butter to about 370 °F, drop in the shrimp (carefully) and cook till they start to brown (about 2 minutes) keeping an eye on the heat. Flip over and sear for about another two minutes.

2. Add the jalapenos, lemongrass, ginger, garlic, pepper flakes, vegetable stock, soy sauce, scallion whites, and barbeque sauce then mix well to combine and cook just a bit more, so things meld some (about a minute). Remove from the heat. Taste and adjust the barbeque sauce if necessary. After plating garnish with the scallion greens.

3. I make Taste of Home's "Easy Fried Rice" with this to add some additional flavor and texture, or any favorite rice dish will work. This dish is also easy to reconstitute for leftovers.

Shrimp and Okra Hoagie

One of my favorite vegetables is fresh okra, which we like roasted, in many types of dishes. Recently I picked up lots of shrimp on sale and had some Italian rolls hanging around, so we figured, let's put all this together. The whole meal can be done on the grill to save on clean up!

Ingredients

- 12 size 16-20 shrimp peeled and deveined
- 4 cloves garlic peeled and chopped
- 1 cup fresh okra sliced
- 4 tbsp peanut oil divided
- 8 shishito peppers
- 2-3 tbsp mayonnaise
- ½ lemon (juice)
- ¼ tsp crushed coriander seeds
- 1 tsp Old Bay hot sauce
- 2 Italian rolls split
- 4 small watermelon slices
- 4-6 leaves Romaine lettuce cored
- 2 tbsp butter
- 1 tbsp olive oil
- Salt and pepper

1. Split the two rolls longways being sure not to break the "hinge". Heat the olive oil in a large pan or griddle, then lay the rolls in, rotating a couple times (it's good to use some weight for consistent browning). Once browned remove and lay on plates.
2. Combine 2 tbsp peanut oil, salt, pepper, and okra in a plastic bag, mix to combine well- place on baking sheet and roast at 400 °F for 25-30 minutes, turning once (until they start to brown). This can be done ahead of time.
3. Combine homemade mayo (recipe in basics), lemon juice, Old bay hot sauce, and coriander then set aside. Add more lemon juice if required to thin. Salt and pepper to taste.
4. Sauté the shishitos in peanut oil (cast iron pan) until the exterior starts to cook, remove from heat and chop.
5. In the same cast iron pan heat the butter to about 350 °F, drop in the shrimp, cook the first side 2-3 minutes (watch the heat and temp), then turn over for another 2-3 minutes, add the garlic in the last minute, stir to combine. Remove from the heat.
6. Sprinkle salt and pepper on each watermelon slice, then grill for about 2 minutes per side, remove and plate.
7. Place Romaine on each roll, followed by the shrimp, okra, shishitos, then drizzle the sauce over top. Cut in half and plate along with watermelon.

Chesapeake Fried Green Tomatoes
and Garlic Shrimp

One of the things I always enjoyed when working or traveling around Baltimore were the multitude of great small restaurants, each with their own twist on what I'd call "down home food" (as Mamaw Johnson used to say)- great meals based on simple ingredients. My favorite stop, "Miss Shirley's Place" has the best fried green tomatoes around and are the inspiration for this dish.

Ingredients

- 2 medium green tomatoes in ¼ inch slices
- 1 lb #16-20 shrimp peeled and deveined
- ½ cup corn meal
- ½ cup AP flour
- 1 tsp Old Bay seasoning
- 2 cups jasmine rice (cooked)
- Corn off 2 grilled cobs
- 3 cloves garlic chopped
- 1 large shallot sliced
- 1-2 eggs
- ¼ cup marsala wine
- 2 tbsp homemade mayonnaise
- ¼ tsp cardamom
- 2 tbsp butter
- ½ tsp salt
- ½ teaspoon pepper
- 2-3 tsp lemon juice
- Peanut oil
- Parsley or cilantro (optional)

1. Place the flour in a medium bowl, then combine the corn meal, Old Bay, salt, and pepper on a flat plate and set aside. Beat the egg (s) in another medium bowl. Dip each slice of tomato first in the flour, then in the eggs, then in the cornmeal mixture, and set on a rack. Combine the mayonnaise, cardamom, and lemon juice in a small bowl and set aside.
2. Heat two tbsp peanut oil in a deep pan, add the shallots and corn, cook until the shallots shine. Next add the marsala wine and cook off, then add the rice and mix. Turn off the heat. Any other vegetables can be added if desired.
3. In a cast iron pan heat about ¼ inch of peanut oil to 370 °F, then cook the tomatoes in batches, turning several times until browned all over, remove to a rack.
4. Drain the oil from the pan (or use another one) and add two tablespoons of butter and heat to 350 °F, then add the shrimp and allow to cook for three minutes on the first side, add the garlic, flip, and another two minutes on the other side.
5. Place the tomatoes on the plates, then the rice, and spoon the garlic shrimp over top of the rice. Drizzle on the lemon cardamom mayo, and garnish with parsley or cilantro.

The Queen's Fish and Chips

After watching several English chefs make their version of "traditional" fish and chips, and "Food Outsider's" quest for England's best version, Carolyn started making her own version using a key local ingredient- "Kiltlifter' Scottish style Ale, added "Old Bay" seasoning, and uses russet potatoes. She stacks them like the Queen liked, and we usually serve with our "Western Mushy Peas".

Ingredients

- 6 oz cod fish
- 1 cup of flour (I use 00 flour or AP flour), and a little more for dusting
- ½ tsp baking powder
- ¼ tsp pepper
- ½ tsp Old Bay Seasoning
- 1 cup cold beer
- 2 Russet Potatoes peeled
- Enough canola oil to cover fries when cooking, about 1 ½ to 2 inches deep
- 2 tbsp homemade mayonnaise
- ½ tsp ground coriander
- 2-3 tsp lemon juice
- Salt and pepper to taste
- Malt vinegar

1. Cut the potatoes into ¼-by-¼ inch fries by cutting ¼" slabs and then cutting them into ¼" strips. Fries should be about 4" long. If the fries are too long, they can be cut in half.
2. Next place the fries into a bowl filled with water and soak for 15-30 minutes. While the potatoes are soaking preheat oil to 375 °F. I use an electric deep fryer with a basket.
3. Cut the cod into 1" x 1" x 3" strips and dry them.
4. Drain the fries and allow them to dry completely, in between two kitchen towels, before putting them in the fryer.
5. Cook the French fries twice, first before the fish for 10-20 minutes, depending on size, drain on rack and cook again after the fish has cooked, 30-60 seconds, until golden brown. Remove to a rack to cool, add salt and pepper to taste.
6. Combine the flour, baking powder, salt, pepper, and Old Bay Seasoning in a bowl, then mix the beer into the dry ingredients well.
7. Dust the cod strips with flour, dip each one into the flour-beer mixture, and place directly in the hot oil. Cook until golden brown (4 -6 minutes), remove, drain on paper towel then plate (the Queen liked hers stacked up). Sprinkle on malt vinegar.
8. Combine the mayonnaise, lemon juice, and coriander in a small bowl, to get a thin sauce like consistency, add salt, and pepper to taste, then spoon over the fish.

Cast Iron Dover Sole

Growing up on the East Coast we ate flounder a lot, a nice flat fish with light taste and good texture. A few years ago we ate some Dover Sole (another flat fish) while vacationing in England, and it was awesome. I can't get flounder here in Arizona, but Dover Sole comes in fresh from the Pacific, so I just give it a dusting of cornmeal, flour, panko, and of course Old Bay, then a quick cook in my trusty cast iron.

Ingredients

- 1 lb fresh Dover sole
- ¾ cup corn meal
- ¼ cup AP flour
- ¼ cup panko breadcrumbs
- 1 tsp Old Bay seasoning
- 2 tbsp homemade mayonnaise
- 2-3 tsp lemon juice
- ½ tsp crushed coriander seeds (or cardamom)
- ½ tsp salt
- ½ tsp pepper
- 3 tbsp butter divided
- 2 tbsp peanut or avocado oil

1. Combine the mayonnaise, coriander and lemon juice in a bowl and mix together until a nice thin consistency is obtained, then set aside.
2. On a large flat plate combine the corn meal, flour, panko, salt, pepper, and Old Bay and mix well. Rinse and then pat the fish dry.
3. In a large cast iron pan heat two tablespoons butter (clarified butter lessens the splatter) and one tablespoon oil to around 375 °F. Keep the heat up while cooking.
4. Dredge the first batch of filets in the cornmeal mixture, place carefully in the pan and cook two-three minutes (depending on the size of each piece), then turn and cook the other side for an additional two-three minutes until browned.
5. Repeat the process until all the fish has been cooked, add the remaining butter and oil as required, draining each batch on paper towels.
6. Plate the fish and drizzle the sauce over top. My favorite side with this dish is fried green tomatoes, followed by hush puppies or a nice root vegetable mash.

Seared Squid Steak

The first time I had squid steaks was in San Diego while in the Marine Corps, after myself and a couple friends had gone sailing with an older gentlemen, and then had lunch. This is a recipe I have previously done with Halibut, however squid steak is a much more affordable option, tastes great, and doesn't take long to make. We usually have these with some type of mashed root vegetables, and the quick mushroom sauce provides a nice earthy flavor.

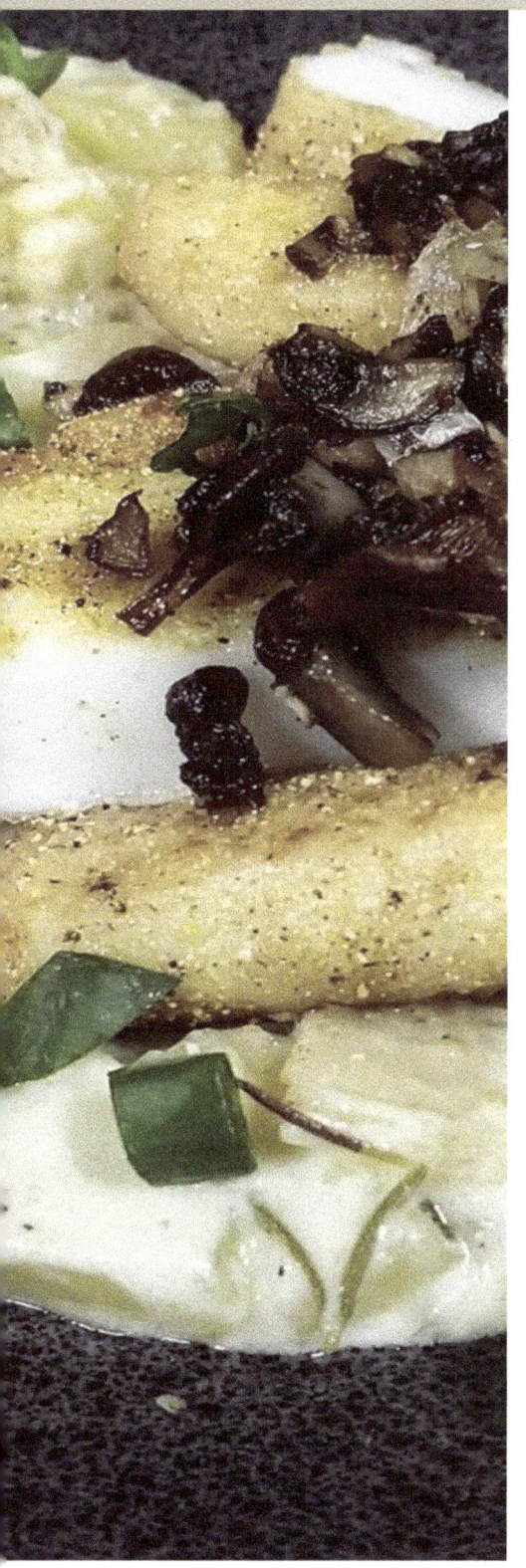

Ingredients

- 2 squid steaks (5-6 oz.) defrosted
- 2 pieces pancetta chopped
- 4 oz portabella mushrooms chopped
- 1-2 oz dried chanterelle mushrooms chopped
- 2 green onions chopped
- Lemon juice
- ¼ cup sherry
- ½ cup duck stock (or similar)
- ½ jalapeno chopped
- 1 clove garlic minced
- ¼ cup corn meal
- ¼ cup flour
- ¼ cup panko breadcrumbs
- 1 tsp Old Bay seasoning
- 2 tbsp butter
- 2 tbsp peanut or avocado oil
- ½ tsp salt
- ½ tsp pepper

1. Combine the corn meal, flour, panko, old bay, salt, and pepper on a plate and mix well. Dry off the squid steaks and coat them well in the mixture then set aside. Rehydrate the chanterelles for a few minutes.

2. In a small saucepan add one tbsp oil, shallots, jalapeno, mushrooms and cook a few minutes until the mushrooms sweat. Next add the sherry, cook for another minute, then add the duck stock and garlic, bring to a boil, simmer to reduce by 25%.

3. Once the sauce is finished, drop the butter and remaining oil into a cast iron pan with pancetta and allow to heat to 375 °F. Drop the squid steaks in and cook for about three minutes, then turn over and cook another three minutes (or until browned) watch the heat in the pan. Turn again, if necessary, remove from pan, rest for several minutes then slice.

4. Spoon some potatoes onto each plate, lay the sliced squid steak on top, then add the sauce. Garnish with a squeeze of lemon juice and the chopped green onions.

Pork Butt Bonanza

Every time I'm in the market in town is an opportunity to find on sale "specials" for many of our staple items, especially on meats, fish, and shellfish. We can then take a look at the Playbook and lay out several meals easily, or freeze for later, so we don't miss the deal.

Every so often Pork Shoulder also known as "Boston Butt", will be reduced by one half to two thirds in price, so we always buy two. One for now and one for later.

We break up the pork into the portions required for our favorites like 10th Street Pork or Bourbon Pulled Pork, then grind up the remainder for breakfast sausage or non spiced ground pork, for Lion's Head Meatballs, Meatloaf or Meatballs (with fennel added), Biscuits and Sausage Gravy, or Sausage Egg and Cheese sandwiches known as "The Southwark", and recently for Eggrolls, Skillet Stir Fry and Cubanos.

The long list of meal ideas available for pork shoulder shows how versatile this cut of meat is, especially when its purchased "on sale".

BJ's Ground Pork

Grinding your own pork is a wonderful way to make many different meals with one pork shoulder (Boston Butt). Our recipe is inspired by Alton Brown's "Breakfast Sausage" recipe, which has been handed down through several generations. The best things about grinding your own pork are no added fat, and no artificial ingredients or preservatives. It's relatively lean and all the small pieces or scraps get used. Lots of flavors can be added so it's like a blank food canvas!

Ingredients

- 2 lbs pork shoulder cold
- 2 tsp salt
- 2 tsp pepper
- 4 tsp sage leaves chopped fine
- 2 tsp rosemary chopped fine
- 1 tbsp dark brown sugar
- ½ tsp ground nutmeg
- ½ tsp cayenne pepper
- ½ tsp pepper flakes
- ¼ tsp ground cloves
- 1 tbsp maple natural syrup
- ½ tsp fennel seeds (optional)

1. Chop the pork into ½" cubes and combine with remaining ingredients in a large bowl, mix well to combine. Allow to set for 30 minutes or so. I add the fennel for meatloaf.
2. Set up your grinder, put hearing protection on, and run the pork mixture through, capturing it in a resealable container as it comes out. Be sure to unplug the grinder immediately when finished!
3. Store the finished ground pork in the refrigerator for up to a five days.
4. I will normally run a pound or two through without seasoning (for meatballs, egg rolls or stir fry) then run the seasoned meat next.

10th Street Roast Pork Sandwich

Back in the 80's and 90's in South Philadelphia, one of my favorite lunches was an Italian Pork sandwich, at D'Nicks down near 10th and Oregon. The sandwich was just sopping wet in an awesome gravy, the pork was super tender, with fresh provolone and hot cherry peppers. My recipe uses Amoroso rolls we ship in from the East, our homemade vegetable stock, along with sauteed garlic spinach.

Ingredients

- 1 lb pork shoulder
- 1 sprig rosemary
- 2 cloves of garlic, chopped
- 2 cups of vegetable stock (homemade if possible)
- ½ cup plus 2 tbsp Marsala wine divided
- 2 handfuls of fresh spinach
- 1 tsp local honey
- 1 shallot chopped
- ½ tsp fennel seeds
- ½ tsp hot pepper flakes
- 2 tbsp olive oil
- ½ tsp salt
- ½ tsp pepper
- 2 Italian Rolls split
- 6-8 slices of Provolone cheese
- Hot cherry peppers

1. Preheat oven to 275° F.
2. Put the pork shoulder, rosemary, 1 clove garlic, stock, 1/2 cup wine, pepper flakes, fennel, honey, salt, and pepper into a Dutch oven and heat it up to just boiling.
3. Move the Dutch oven into the oven and cook for 2.5-3 hours turning every 30 minutes hours until the meat temperature is at least 145 °F. Pull the pork apart in the Dutch oven and mix with the gravy.
4. Once the pork is nearly done, sweat the shallot in olive oil in a non-stick pan, then drop in 2 tbsp of marsala. Next add the spinach, remaining garlic, and salt and pepper and cover for about one minute. Remove the cover and cook until the spinach just wilts. (Broccoli rabe can be substituted for spinach).
5. Toast the Italian rolls on a griddle or large pan with olive oil, plate, and place provolone slices on the bread.
6. Using tongs place some pork on each roll and ladle some juices on top. Next add the spinach, then chop two hot cherry peppers and sprinkle on top. Cut in half and serve. Feel free to spoon on more gravy!

Lion's Head Meatballs and Leftovers

A fresh pork shoulder makes great sausage, both seasoned and unseasoned. I like to use the unseasoned for this dish, which is inspired by Cook's Illustrated January/February 2020 featured dish. We updated the broth to include some of our favorite ingredients, which really elevates the flavor. This is great for leftovers, and can be repurposed in several ways.

Ingredients

- ¾ tsp baking soda
- ½ tsp salt
- 2 lbs ground pork
- 1 egg, lightly beaten
- 2 scallions, white parts minced, green parts sliced thin
- 2 tbsp plus 1 tsp soy sauce
- 2 tbsp Sake
- 4 tsp sugar
- 2 tsp grated fresh ginger
- ½ tsp white pepper
- 4 cups homemade vegetable stock
- 1 tsp miso paste
- 1 tsp gochujang
- 1 tbsp mirin
- ¼ tsp sesame oil
- 1 small head of Napa cabbage (1 ½ lbs.) quartered lengthwise, cored and cut crosswise into 2-inch pieces
- 4 oz Pad Thai rice noodles
- ½ tsp sesame seeds

1. Adjust oven rack to lower-middle position and preheat oven to 325 °F.
2. Whisk baking soda, salt, and 2 tbsp water together in a stand mixer bowl.
3. Add pork to baking soda mixture, then toss to combine.
4. Add egg, scallion whites, 2 tbsp soy sauce, Sake, ginger, sugar, and white pepper to the bowl.
5. Fit stand mixer with paddle and beat on medium speed until mixture is well combined and has stiffened and started to pull away from the sides of the bowl and pork has slightly lightened in color, 45 to 60 seconds.
6. Using wet hands, form about ½ cup (4.5 oz) pork mixture into 3-inch round meatball; repeat with remaining mixture to form 8 meatballs.

Lion's Head Meatballs and Leftovers
Continued

7. Put the stock in a Dutch oven then and add miso, mirin, 1 tsp soy sauce, sesame oil, and gochujang, bring to a boil then remove from the heat. Next place the meatballs in the broth with one in the center and seven around it. The meatballs will not be totally submerged.

8. Cover and put Dutch oven into the oven and cook for about one hour.

9. Transfer meatballs to a large plate. Add cabbage to the Dutch oven in an even layer and arrange meatballs on cabbage, paler side up. Cover, return Dutch oven to the oven and continue to cook until meatballs are lightly browned, and cabbage is softened, about 30 min longer.

10. While the meatballs and cabbage cook, bring 2 quarts of water to boil in a large pot and cook the rice noodles according to the directions on the package.

11. Place the cooked rice noodles into large soup bowls then ladle in the meatballs, cabbage, and broth. Sprinkle with scallion greens and sesame seeds and serve.

One of my favorite leftovers is to slice the Lions Head meatballs in half, sauté in a skillet until both sides are brown, then drop in a quick miso gochujang broth and cook for a couple minutes. These can be used with many sides like rice, noodles, or my favorite seared sushi rice sticks.

The Southwark
Sausage, Egg, and Cheese Sandwich

Back when I used to work at the Southwark generating station (where the S. S. United States was docked), there was a small shop that sold several types of breakfast sandwiches every morning. Those hot sandwiches really took the edge off a cold, foggy, Delaware River morning!

Ingredients

- 6-8 oz BJ's Ground Pork (or similar)
- 2 Italian rolls split
- 3-4 oz grated cheddar and pepper-jack cheese
- 3 eggs
- ¼ cup half and half
- 1–2 tbsp olive oil
- Spray avocado oil
- 2 cherry peppers cored chopped
- 2-3 tbsp Johnson's barbeque sauce (or personal choice)

1. Form the ground pork into two rectangular pieces and cook in a avocado oil sprayed non-stick pan at medium low heat, turning often, until browned. Remove from the pan, drain on paper towel, then cut each in half lengthwise.

2. While the pork is cooking, split the two rolls longways, (don't break the "hinge"). Heat up a wide pan, add the olive oil and lay in the rolls rotating a couple times (use a weight if available). Once browned, plate.

3. Whisk the eggs with half and half then pour into a wide preheated pan (I use the same pan that the rolls were browned in). Allow to cook until they start to stiffen, add the cheese across the center, and once the edges start to brown flip one side towards the center, then the other side over top. Turn off the heat.

4. Spoon the barbeque sauce on both sides of each roll, place 2 half pieces of ground pork on one side of the roll, then cut the omelet in half at the center and again longways (I just use my spatula in the pan). Place two sections of omelet on each roll, keeping the ends facing inside. Salt and pepper to taste, add the cherry peppers, cut in half, and serve.

JB's Meatballs and Red Sauce

One dish I like to use our fresh ground pork shoulder in is meatballs with red sauce. This version is inspired by watching Joe Bastianich, so they are roasted then finished in the sauce, perfect with pasta, or broken up for Pomodoro sauce, but our real favorite is on a meatball sandwich with fresh provolone!

Ingredients

Sauce

- 28 oz can San Marzano peeled tomatoes crushed
- 15 oz can fire roasted diced tomatoes
- 29 oz can tomato sauce
- 2 tsp brown sugar
- 1 tbsp molasses
- ½ tsp pepper flakes
- 4 tbsp olive oil

Meatballs

- ½ lb ground beef
- ½ lb home ground pork
- ½ red pepper chopped finely
- ½ medium onion finely chopped
- 1 jalapeno cored and chopped
- 3 cloves garlic minced
- 2 tsp Worcestershire sauce
- ½ cup half and half
- ¼ cup panko breadcrumbs
- ¼ cup breadcrumbs
- ¼ tsp fennel seeds
- 1 tbsp olive oil

1. In a Dutch oven combine the sauce ingredients and bring to a slow boil stirring regularly, then simmer until the meatballs are added. Watch the heat and stir often so the bottom doesn't burn.

2. Heat one tbsp olive oil in a nonstick pan then drop in the onion, jalapeno, and red pepper. Cook until the onions start to soften, then drop in the garlic, cook another minute, and remove from the heat. Set the oven to 400 °F.

3. Place the ground pork, ground beef, Worcestershire, fennel, panko, and breadcrumbs, into a large mixing bowl. Drop in the cooked vegetables and the half and half. Combine and mix well, but do not overmix. Divide the meat mixture into 6 equal balls (I use a scale) and place them into a lightly oiled 13' x9" glass baking dish, then place in the oven, center rack. Cook for between 25 and 30 minutes, turning once.

4. Once meatballs are browned remove from the baking dish, place in the sauce, stir to cover. Simmer an additional 10-15 minutes, then they are ready to serve.

Biscuits and Sausage Gravy

As a kid, I'd eat this dish traveling South to visit Mamaw Johnson, usually at a "Stuckeys", and at Uncle George's house in Arkansas. I use our breakfast sausage, and Carolyn makes jalapeno biscuits from the "Essential Emeril" cookbook, which are perfect for this. Louisiana hot sauce provides a nice vinegar kick.

Ingredients

- 6 oz BJs ground pork
- 3 homemade jalapeno biscuits (or similar)
- 1 and ½ cup milk
- 3 tbsp butter
- 3 tbsp AP flour
- 1 tbsp avocado oil
- 1 tbsp Louisiana Hot Sauce

1. Cut each biscuit in half, place on heated griddle or pan and brown, heat up the other side also. Place 3 biscuits browned sides up on two plates.

2. Heat the oil in a wide nonstick pan, drop in the sausage and cook for about 5 minutes, until it starts to brown slightly, breaking it apart as it cooks.

3. Once the pork is done remove from the pan and set aside, lower the heat, then add the butter, stirring it while it melts. Next add the flour and mix with the butter, then slowly stir in the milk raising the heat slightly.

4. Continue to cook the sauce stirring often for about 4 minutes, (the center will start to bubble,) then add the pork back in and mix together well. Stop the cooking process before it seems done as it will thicken up as it cools. I don't add salt or pepper since it's in the pork, so check here, and adjust as necessary.

5. Spoon the gravy onto the biscuits, then drizzle on some hot sauce and its done.

Emeril's biscuits are found on page 51 of "Essential Emeril", which we have modified to include 1 tsp of brown sugar, more buttermilk, and bake at 425 °F rather than 375 °F.

Mountain View Meatloaf and Leftovers

One thing we make after breaking down a pork shoulder is ground pork, without the added fat, which is perfect for meatloaf when combined with beef or bison. This recipe three meals for us, first with Pennsylvania Dutch egg noodles and mushroom marsala sauce or Johnson's barbeque sauce, then with mashed root vegetables and mushroom sauce, and of course with duck fat potatoes and chimichurri!

Ingredients

Meatloaf

- 1 lb BJ's ground pork
- 1 lb ground beef or bison
- 8 oz. PA Dutch egg noodles cooked
- ½ large yellow onion finely chopped
- ½ red pepper finely chopped
- 1 large jalapeno finely chopped
- 4 cloves garlic minced
- 1 egg beaten
- ¾ cup half and half
- ½ cup breadcrumbs
- ¼ cup panko breadcrumbs
- 1 tsp Worcestershire sauce
- 1 tbsp fresh grated horseradish
- ½ tsp fennel seed ground
- 2 tbsp olive oil

1. Heat up a non-stick pan and add the oil, onion, red pepper, jalapeno and allow to sweat till the onions are just opaque. Add the garlic and cook for another minute then remove from the heat.

2. In a large bowl combine the sausage, beef (or bison), egg, breadcrumbs, panko, Worcestershire, fennel, horseradish, and finally the half and half, which should create a "moat" around the other ingredients.

3. Next add the hot ingredients and mix to combine minimally. The meat mixture should be loose and creamy looking.

4. Place the mixture in a 9'X13' baking dish (glass preferred) and spread out to a depth of about ¾ inch. Place in a preheated 375 °F oven for about 45 minutes, watching for it to "tighten up" then remove from the oven and rest for 10 minutes.

5. Plate one third and refrigerate the rest for leftovers.

Continued...

Ingredients

Sauce

- 2 tbsp marsala wine
- ½ tsp molasses
- ½ tsp brown sugar
- 1 cup beef stock
- 1 large shallot finely chopped
- ½ tsp hot sauce
- 3-4 oz baby Bellas chopped
- 4 oz dehydrated porcini and chanterelle mushrooms
- 1 tbsp olive oil
- 2 tbsp butter

1. While the meatloaf is cooking, in a small pot add the olive oil, allow to heat up, then add the shallots and mushrooms and cook for about 5 minutes stirring often. Next drop in the marsala and cook for another minute, then add the stock, molasses, brown sugar, and hot sauce, mix to combine and cook down by about 30 percent, stirring often. Once reduced add the butter and stir until well incorporated. Turn off the heat.
2. Divide the cooked noodles between two plates, then take about 1/3rd of the meatloaf out of the baking dish to a cutting board, cut cross ways into ½"- ¾" sections and lay over the noodles, then spoon the sauce over both plates and serve.
3. For leftover meatloaf and noodles, I heat the meat up at 350 °F for about 8 -10 minutes, reduce about ½ cup of Johnson's barbeque sauce by 25% or so in a saucepan. For the noodles drop 2 tbsp oil, 1 finely chopped shallot, and heat in deep pan, then drop in 2 handfuls of kale, some white balsamic, and 2 cloves of minced garlic - cover for two minutes, mix, and then add the noodles and 2 tbsp of butter- cook on low until heated through.
4. The second leftover option uses "Smashed Root Vegetables" (in the "Sides" section) for the side, I just reconstitute the mushroom sauce (or make new), or use reduced Johnson's barbeque sauce, either one is great.
5. The third variation of this dish utilizes our "Duck Fat Potatoes" (from the "Sides" section) and your favorite chimichurri recipe, we use a version of Mirta Rinaldi's recipe which uses cilantro (50%) with the parsley and white balsamic vinegar (Food and Wine, September 2021, page 42) but any personal favorite is fine. This version might be my favorite.

8 Minute Egg Rolls

After our only local Chinese takeout restaurant closed, we had to come up with a new alternative. This recipe uses our home ground pork, and are great as a side or by themselves. The remainer are wrapped and frozen in sets of two for later, then reheated in the air fryer in about 8 minutes when needed.

Ingredients

- 20 egg roll wrappers (Twin Dragon or similar)
- 1 lb BJs ground pork
- ½ head green cabbage chopped
- 2 large carrots peeled and grated
- 2 spring onions chopped
- 8 oz can water chestnuts chopped
- 3 cloves garlic minced
- 2 tbsp fresh ginger minced
- 2 tbsp oyster sauce
- 1 tsp gochujang
- 1 tsp mirin
- ½ tsp sesame oil
- ½ tsp pepper flakes
- 1-2 eggs beaten
- Peanut oil

1. Combine the oyster sauce, gochujang, sesame oil, mirin, and pepper flakes, set aside.
2. In a large cast iron pan cook the pork until its done, remove from pan.
3. Drop the carrots and onions in the same pan, cook 3-5 minutes, then add the cabbage and cover- cook about 6-8 minutes stirring often, then add the ginger, garlic, water chestnuts, followed by the wet ingredients from step 1, add the pork back in, then cook a few more minutes.
4. Place about 2 tbsp of the mixture in each wrapper, then fold up from the bottom, pinch and close the sides (like a Christmas present) brush egg on the inside and close the last flap. Place in fryer preheated to 375 °F for about 2-3 minutes, flip once for another couple minutes until browned, then drain on a rack.
5. Place the egg rolls on a sheet pan and place in freezer overnight, so they freeze solid. I usually cook 4 then freeze the rest in 2 piece packs for later.
6. To reheat, set the air fryer to 375 and cook for 4 minutes on the first side, turn and another 4 on the other side.
7. We use the "Woks Of Life" sweet and sour sauce recipe since it doesn't use any ketchup.

Bourbon Pulled Pork

Whenever Carolyn makes shrimp tacos, there is always plenty of cabbage and apple slaw leftover, so we needed a dish to use this up. Tareq Taylor's pulled pork recipe inspired me to take a shot at my own version, which is super easy to make, has a nice smoky taste, with a deep sweet heat background flavor.

Ingredients

- 1 lb pork shoulder
- 1 can (8 oz) tomato paste
- 1 tsp chili powder
- ½ tsp cayenne
- ½ tsp garlic powder
- ½ tsp onion powder
- 1 tbsp brown sugar
- 2 tsp molasses
- 2 tbsp cider vinegar
- 2 oz bourbon
- Warm water
- 1 tbsp avocado oil
- 4 Artesian or tailgater rolls
- Leftover Asian Slaw (from "Seared Garlic Shrimp Tacos" in Seafood Section) or similar

1. In a 16 ounce measuring cup (2 cups) combine everything except the pork and water and mix well. Then add water up to the 2 cup line. Heat the oven to 320F.

2. In a small Dutch oven heat the oil to about 350 °F, then brown the pork on all sides. Next add the 2 cups of spice mixture and turn the pork a few times in it as it comes to a boil, then place in oven for 2-3 hours. Once it can be broken apart remove from the oven and break up to combine with the sauce.

3. Brown the rolls on a griddle or on the grill (preferred), place bottom on plates, followed by the pork, then slaw, followed by the top bun.

4. The Asian Slaw recipe is part of our "Seared Garlic Shrimp Tacos" recipe in the Seafood Section.

Hamamania

Sales after holidays on ham can be as much as 60% off, especially with a preferred shopper card. However, watch for brands that add water, brine or chemicals.

We challenge ourselves to only use what we have in the house, utilize the Playbook, and stretch this as far as we can ("the $13 Dollar Ham Challenge"), which saves us a ton of money!

In the past, I always baked the ham as directed, but they came out really dry. Now, it goes into a 325F oven (after coming to room temperature), in a roasting pan with 16 oz of ginger ale on the bottom and a cover, checking the temperature every hour or 40 minutes until it gets to 120F- then it comes out to rest.

While cooking we make our chipotle honey mustard ham sauce (I don't glaze the exterior), and our first sides are normally some type of root vegetables, vegetable corn rice, vegetable orzo, or duck fat potatoes, all inexpensive and great for leftovers.

Honey Mustard Chipotle Sauce

Over the years we've tried different techniques for saucing or glazing a baked ham, and finally developed one with a nice depth of flavor and consistency. However, we don't use it as exterior glaze, but as a sauce when it's been plated or on sandwiches.

Ingredients

- 1 tbsp avocado oil
- 1 shallot chopped
- 2 tbsp white wine
- ½ cup vegetable stock
- 2 tsp Dijon mustard
- 1 tbsp chopped chipotle peppers in adobo sauce
- 2 tsp brown sugar
- 1 tbsp honey
- 2 tbsp apple juice
- 1 tbsp butter
- Salt and pepper to taste

1. Heat the avocado oil in a saucepan over medium heat.
2. Add shallots and cook until softened, 1-2 min.
3. Pour in wine and cook off alcohol for 2 min.
4. Add vegetable stock, mustard, chipotle peppers, brown sugar, honey, and apple juice. Bring to a boil then lower heat to medium low and simmer uncovered for 20 minutes to thicken.
5. Add butter and cook for 4 - 5 more minutes, then add salt and pepper to taste.

Leftover sauce can be stored in the refrigerator for later.

Ham Egg and Cheese Hoagie

Breakfast sandwiches on Italian rolls are one of my favorites, especially with leftovers like on sale ham. We normally make our marinated grilled pineapple along with a baked ham, so why not put them together in a hoagie, then add eggs and cheese, and you have a great breakfast sandwich.

Ingredients

- 5-6 ounces left over ham slices
- 2 Italian rolls split
- 2-2.5 oz grated pepperjack cheese
- 1 jalapeno cored and chopped
- 4-5 oz grilled pineapple
- 3 eggs
- ¼ cup half and half
- 2-3 tbsp olive oil
- 3 tbsp Johnson's barbeque sauce (or similar) or leftover honey chipotle mustard sauce
- Spray avocado oil

1. Split two rolls longways, keeping the hinge intact. Heat 1 tbsp olive oil in a wide pan and brown the rolls cut-side down (use a weight for even browning), rotating twice, about 3 min. Place on plates, browned side up.
2. Heat 1 tbsp avocado oil or spray in another pan to 350° F, cook the ham slices 1-2 min per side until lightly browned. Turn off heat, add pineapple with juice, and stir. Do this while the eggs are cooking.
3. Whisk 4 eggs with 2 tbsp half-and-half, pour into a pre-heated wide pan (I wipe out and reuse the roll pan) on medium-low. Cook until the top sets, 4-5 min. Add the cheese and chopped jalapenos across the center. When the edges brown, fold the first side to center, then the second side over top ,turn off heat.
4. Spread the barbecue or mustard sauce on each roll, cut the omelet in half crosswise, then longways into four pieces. Place two pieces of omelet per roll, ends facing inward, top with the ham-pineapple mix using tongs. cut in half, and serve.

Grilled Ham and Avocado Sandwich

One sandwich we enjoy is our "HLT", which is a ham, lettuce and tomato sandwich, that includes avocado, jalapeno, and chipotle mayonnaise for some kick. I usually make it with 21 grain bread, but rye is fine too, along with morning food favorites like homemade beet pickled eggs and onions.

Ingredients

- 5 -7 oz leftover ham in slices
- 1 avocado seeded, peeled, and sliced longways
- 2 beet pickled eggs
- Sliced pickled beets and onions
- 1 large tomato sliced and cored (if necessary)
- 3 leaves Romaine lettuce cored
- 1 medium jalapeno sliced
- 1 tbsp lime juice
- 4 slices 21 grain bread (or Jewish Rye)
- 1-2 tbsp homemade mayonnaise
- 1 tsp crushed chipotle with adobo sauce
- 1 tbsp butter

1. Cook the ham, turning often, until it's just browned on both sides and remove from the heat. Mix the chipotle and mayonnaise together in a small bowl and set aside. Squeeze the lime juice over the avocado slices and salt and pepper to taste.

2. Melt the butter on a griddle and drop on the bread slices- turning a couple of times until both sides are nicely browned turn off the heat, move to plates.

3. Lay the avocado pieces on the bottom pieces of bread and "smush" down with a fork, then the jalapeno slices. Next cover with the Romaine leaves torn or cut to fit, lay on the tomatoes as level as possible, then add the ham across the top.

4. Cover the upper bread slices on the inside with chipotle mayonnaise and place it on top, pressing down to keep everything together, cut in half and plate, garnish the plate with the eggs, beets, and onions.

5. Our beet pickled egg recipe and mayonnaise recipe are both in the "Basics" section of the LOR Playbook.

Ham, Pickled Apple, and Onion Pizza

One of the things we like to pair with ham is pickled apples and onions, which is inspired by Nordic cuisine. Of course we add jalapeno into the mix, then drop it all onto a Napoli style pizza. The sweet and sour pickled vegetables work great with the salty ham, a really nice dish!

Ingredients

- 12 oz pizza dough homemade (Basics Section) or store bought
- 14 oz peeled San Marzano tomatoes lightly crushed (1/2 can)
- 4 oz mozzarella cheese chopped finely
- 6-7 oz leftover ham pieces
- 1 apple peeled, cored, and thinly sliced
- 1 jalapeno thinly sliced
- ½ red onion thinly sliced
- ⅓ cup organic sugar
- ⅓ cup apple cider vinegar
- ⅔ cup water
- Semolina flour for dusting
- Ricotta cheese (optional)

1. Combine the sugar, vinegar, and water in a medium bowl and stir until most of the sugar dissolves, then add the onions, jalapenos, and apples mix well and set aside for about 30 minutes, mixing a couple more times. Drain the mixture before it goes on the pizza.

2. Make the dough or use store bought, about 12 ounces is required for a 13-inch pizza. Roll out the dough, then place on a peel sprinkled with semolina. Heat oven to 450 °F and allow pizza steel (or stone) to heat for 20-30 minutes while preparing the pizza.

3. Spread the San Marzano tomatoes around the crust to cover, then add the ham, followed by apples, onions, and jalapenos, and finally add the mozzarella over top. (If we have Ricotta on hand, I'll add several small dollops around the pizza as well).

4. Carefully slide the pizza off the peel and onto the pizza steel (this is always the tricky part!) and bake for about 12-14 minutes, turning 90 degrees a couple times as it cooks, until the top of the cheese begins to brown.

5. Once browned remove from the oven and allow to sit for several minutes, cut into pieces, and serve.

Jalapeno Mac and Cheese with Ham

Home-made mac and cheese is real comfort food. We make this to go along with "On-Sale" ham, and add in lots of those small leftover ham bits, so they don't go to waste. Making it at home allows us to use any combination of our favorite cheeses, along with fresh jalapenos for some kick.

Ingredients

- 8 oz (½ box) of Elbow or Cellentani pasta
- ¼ cup butter
- ¼ cup all-purpose flour
- ½ tsp salt
- ¼ tsp ground black pepper to taste
- 2 cups whole milk
- 2 cups of shredded cheese (mix of Cheddar, Gruyere and/or Fontina)
- 1-2 jalapenos chopped
- ½ cup Panko breadcrumbs
- 1-15 oz can stewed tomatoes
- 1 tsp brown sugar
- 1 tsp molasses

Optional: 1 cup of diced/chopped ham pieces; 1 tsp hot sauce or pepper flakes.

1. Cook the pasta according to the directions on the box so it is firm to the bite, drain.
2. While the pasta is cooking, heat the stewed tomatoes, brown sugar, and molasses in small pan, at low boil for about 8 minutes, mix well to combine. Set aside.
3. Melt the butter in a 10" or 12" cast iron pan over medium heat, then whisk in flour, salt, and pepper until smooth, about 5 minutes.
4. Slowly pour milk into the butter-flour mixture while continuously stirring until the mixture is smooth and bubbling, about 5 minutes, then mix the hot sauce in (optional).
5. Remove heat and add the shredded cheese and jalapeno to the milk mixture, then stir until the cheese is melted, about 3 minutes.
6. Fold the cooked pasta and ham into the cheese mixture until it is coated.
7. Put a layer of Panko breadcrumbs on top of the mac and cheese mixture, place the cast iron pan under the broiler until it is browned, about 2-3 minutes, remove and let stand about 15 minutes before serving. Serve topped with the stewed tomatoes and it's done!

Ham Mac and Cheese Pizza

Carolyn makes awesome macaroni and cheese, which is great alongside a nice "on sale" ham. Personally, I like stewed tomatoes on top, kind of old school I guess! We like to add Mac and Cheese leftovers to our "classic" Napoli style pizza, along with fresh spinach and mushrooms.

Ingredients

- 12 oz pizza dough homemade (Basics Section) or store bought
- 12 oz peeled San Marzano tomatoes lightly crushed
- 6-8 oz leftover mac and cheese
- 5 ounces left over ham pieces
- 2 good handfuls fresh baby spinach
- 4 oz mushrooms sliced
- 2 tbsp good olive oil
- Semolina flour for dusting

1. Make the dough or use store bought, about 12 ounces is required for a 13-inch pizza. Roll out the dough, then place on a peel sprinkled with semolina. Heat oven to 450 °F and allow pizza steel (or stone) to heat for at least 30 minutes, while preparing the pizza.

2. Spread the San Marzano tomatoes around the crust to cover, then add the spinach, followed by the mushrooms, and finally drop on the mac and cheese and ham pieces. Place on pizza steel (or stone) and bake for about 12-14 minutes, turning 90 degrees a couple times as it cooks, until the top of the cheese begins to brown.

3. Once browned remove from the oven and allow to sit for several minutes, drizzle on the olive oil, cut into pieces and serve.

Ham Mac and Cheese Fajita

Mac and Cheese is one side we always make with a baked ham, and there's always leftovers that can be repurposed into fajitas. Our version includes marinated fresh tomatoes, onions, and chiles for heat, along with the sweet grilled pineapple to create a well-rounded flavor, it's easy and tastes great!

Ingredients

- 6 oz leftover ham chopped
- 8-12 oz leftover mac and cheese
- ½ red onion sliced/chopped
- 3-4 oz leftover grilled pineapple chopped
- 1 avocado seeded and quartered
- 1-2 roma tomatoes cored and chopped
- 2 tbsp red wine vinegar
- Juice of 1 lime
- 2 large tortillas (8 or 10 inch)
- 4 oz diced green chiles (1 can)
- ¼ cup "Johnson's Barbeque Sauce" (optional)
- 1 chopped jalapeno (optional)
- 2-3 tbsp avocado or peanut oil for cooking

1. Heat the tortillas in a flat cast iron pan, turning often, till they harden up, then plate. Start heating up a large cast iron pan. Sprinkle the red wine vinegar over the chopped tomatoes and set aside. Place the avocado pieces on each plate, cover with lime juice, then salt and pepper to taste.

2. Heat the oil to about 300 °F in second cast iron pan then drop in the onions and jalapeno and cook till they soften, about 4 minutes. Next add the pineapple and cook another 1-2 minutes, followed by the ham and cook an additional two minutes. Stir often.

3. Clear the center of the pan, spoon in the mac and cheese, pour the chiles on top, then cook for about 2 minutes to warm up. Add the barbeque sauce and mix around with the vegetables.

4. Using tongs place the vegetables onto the tortillas, followed by the mac and cheese/chiles, then cover with the marinated tomatoes.

Hambone Corn Chowder

Every time we make an on sale ham we challenge ourselves to stretch it out and only use ingredients available in the pantry. In the spirit of not wasting anything, the ham bone and all those little pieces that are hard to use, are made into a homemade corn chowder that is perfect for cold mornings.

Ingredients

- 1 ham bone
- 4 cups vegetable broth
- 2 bay leaves
- 1 tbsp butter
- 1 tbsp olive oil
- 1 onion chopped
- 1 shallot chopped
- 2 large Yukon potato peeled and chopped
- 2 carrots chopped
- 2-3 stalks of celery chopped
- 1 jalapeno chopped
- ½ red pepper chopped
- Kernels from 1 ear of grilled corn, or 1 can
- 1 leek white part chopped
- 2 garlic cloves, minced
- 1 tbsp fresh parsley chopped
- ½ cup heavy cream or half and half
- ½ cup sherry or Marsala
- 1 tsp Tabasco Chipotle hot sauce
- 2 cans of creamed corn
- 1 sprig thyme
- 2 sage leaves chopped
- 1 cup ham chopped

1. In a Dutch oven, add butter, oil, onion, shallot, potato, carrot, celery, jalapeno, and red pepper then cook on medium heat until softened. Add corn kernels, leek, and garlic then cook for 1-2 minutes more.
2. Add the sherry and cook for about 5 minutes to cook off the alcohol.
3. Add the 4 cups of broth in and the ham bone. Add bay leaves and water until bone is halfway covered. Bring to a boil, then reduce heat and simmer until very fragrant, about an hour. Remove and discard bone.
4. Add the parsley, cream, hot sauce, creamed corn, thyme, and sage, then simmer for an hour on low heat.
5. Add cooked ham and cook for 5 minutes, then remove from heat and serve. Leftover soup can be portioned and frozen for later.

Pizza and Pasta

Pizza and Calzone Dough

After a long search for New York style pizza outside the East Coast, we tried store bought fresh dough, but it still didn't work for us. We finally found a recipe that works every time and is not complicated. I use this dough for all our pizzas and calzones- it will stay fresh in the refrigerator for a couple days if necessary.

Ingredients

- 1 package (0.25 oz or 2 ¼ tsp) active dry yeast
- 1 tsp granulated sugar
- 1 cup of warm water (110 to 115 °F)
- 2 ½ cups bread flour
- 2 tbsp olive oil
- 1 tsp salt

Chef Rider's
Quick and Easy Pizza Crust

1. Mix yeast, sugar and water into a stand mixer bowl and let stand for 10 minutes until creamy, to proof.
2. Add flour, salt, and oil. Beat with a dough hook until smooth.
3. Form into a ball and put into an oiled bowl, cover to rest for one hour.
4. Turn out dough onto a lightly floured surface and divide dough into 2 balls for two pizzas or 6 balls for calzones, yielding approximately 24 oz of dough.
5. Store unused dough ball in plastic bag with olive oil drizzled in.

Make Ahead Pasta Sauce

It's every man for himself when Carolyn has to work early. So I spend part of the day prior making some vegetable meat pasta sauce and boil a pound of whatever pasta we have in the cabinet, then reheat it "Pomodoro" style each morning over several days (along with a nice piece of grilled Italian bread). It's quick and easy to make, eat, and clean up.

Ingredients

- 28 oz can San Marzano peeled tomatoes crushed
- 28 oz can tomato sauce
- 15 oz can fire roasted diced tomatoes
- 4 tbsp olive oil
- 2 tsp molasses
- 2 tsp dark brown sugar
- 3 cloves garlic minced
- 8 oz ground beef, pork, or Italian sausage
- 4 oz mushrooms chopped
- ½ red pepper finely chopped
- ½ medium onion finely chopped
- ¼ cup marsala wine
- Handful of fresh basil
- Spinach or kale (optional)

1. In a Dutch oven mash the San Marzano tomatoes with a hand blender or potato masher, then pour the cans of tomatoes in and add the molasses, brown sugar, 4 tbsp olive oil, bring to a boil stirring often then simmer for 1-2 hours, occasionally stirring.

2. In a wide sauté pan, cook the meat until almost done, remove from the pan and add the mushrooms, cook for a few minutes, then add the onions and peppers, salt, and pepper to taste, and continue to cook at medium heat for another few minutes, then add the marsala and cook for two more minutes followed by the garlic at the end. Add the meat back to the pan and stir to combine then add to the sauce and combine. Spinach or kale can also be added to this pan if desired.

3. Add the basil and stir to combine about halfway through the cooking time.

4. Once the sauce is done remove from the heat, place in an airtight container, and store in the refrigerator for later use.

Classic Style Napoli Pizza

Using our homemade pizza dough, we have now created several pizza recipes like white vegetable, barbeque chicken, and others. After doing some research I wanted to make a more classic pizza- like they make in Naples -by using fresh quality ingredients, keeping it simple, and great tasting!

Ingredients

- 12 oz pizza dough homemade or store bought
- 14 oz peeled San Marzano tomatoes lightly crushed (½ can)
- 4 oz ricotta cheese (or mozzarella)
- 1 large tomato or 2-3 Roma tomatoes cored and sliced thin
- 1 tbsp freshly grated Parmesan cheese
- 1 tbsp freshly grated Romano cheese
- ½ cup fresh basil (or 1 handful)
- 2 tbsp good olive oil
- Semolina flour for dusting

1. Make the dough or use store bought, about 12 ounces is required for a 13-inch pizza. Roll out the dough, shape to fit the peel, then place on the peel (sprinkled with semolina). Heat oven to 450 °F and allow pizza steel (or stone) to heat for 20-30 minutes at this temperature (while preparing the pizza).

2. Spread the San Marzano tomatoes around the crust to cover, then add the tomatoes, followed by dollops of ricotta (or mozzarella), and finally sprinkle the Parmesan and Romano on. Place on pizza steel (or stone) and bake for about 12 minutes, turning 90 degrees a couple times as it cooks, until the top of the cheese begins to brown.

3. Once browned remove from the oven and allow to sit for several minutes, drizzle on the olive oil and sprinkle on the fresh basil leaves. Cut into pieces and serve.

Green Tomato Pizza

Tomato season in the high desert is limited, so we usually have green tomatoes near the end of growing season. They are great as fried green tomatoes, and some get pickled for use later, however using them in one of our favorite foods- pizza, really hits the mark, especially when combined with pickled onions and jalapenos.

Ingredients

- 12 oz pizza dough homemade or store bought
- ½ tsp salt
- ½ tsp pepper
- ½ tsp pepper flakes
- 2 large green tomatoes or equivalent sliced thin
- 15 slices stick pepperoni (or equivalent deli style)
- ½ large red onion sliced thin and halved
- 1 large jalapeno sliced
- ⅓ cup apple cider vinegar
- ¼ cup organic raw cane sugar
- ⅓ cup water
- 1 oz Romano cheese freshly grated
- 1 oz Parmesan cheese freshly grated
- 1 tbsp olive oil (for 13" pizza)
- 5-8 dollops ricotta
- Semolina flour for dusting

1. Whisk the apple cider vinegar, sugar, and water together until the sugar dissolves, then add the sliced red onions and sliced jalapenos. Let stand for 30-60 minutes stirring several times before using.

2. Make the dough or use store bought, about 12 ounces is required for a 13-inch pizza. Roll out the dough, shape to fit the peel, then place on the peel (sprinkled with semolina). Heat oven to 450 °F and allow pizza steel (or stone) to heat for 20-30 minutes at this temperature (while preparing the pizza).

3. Spread the pickled onions and jalapenos on first, then add the pepperoni, followed by the green tomatoes, pepper flakes, Parmesan, Romano and finally the ricotta. Spanish chorizo can be substituted for pepperoni.

4. Place the pizza on the pizza steel (or stone) and bake for about 12-14 minutes, turning 90 degrees a couple times as it cooks, until the top of the cheese begins to brown. Remove and allow to sit for several minutes, cut into pieces, and serve.

Spinach and Garlic White Pizza

White pizza was impossible to find out here in the high desert, so we went to work on a homemade recipe. Using our homemade dough, it was easy to put together, using our favorite fresh ingredients , and lots of garlic, it tastes just like Philly. Sometimes I leave the mozzarella off and let the ricotta speak for itself!

Ingredients

- 12 oz pizza dough, homemade or store bought
- 5 cloves garlic peeled and minced
- 2 handfuls fresh baby spinach
- ½ tsp salt
- ½ tsp pepper
- ½ tsp pepper flakes
- 6 oz mozzarella chopped finely (divided)
- 1 large tomato or equivalent sliced thin
- 1 oz. Romano cheese freshly grated
- 1 oz. Parmesan cheese freshly grated
- 1.5 tbsp olive oil (for 13" pizza)
- 5-8 dollops ricotta
- Semolina flour

1. Make the dough or use store bought, about 12 ounces is required for a 13-inch pizza. Roll out the dough, shape to fit the peel, then place on the peel (sprinkled with semolina). Heat oven to 450 °F and allow pizza steel (or stone) to heat about 20 minutes (while preparing the pizza).

2. Spread olive oil on first, then sprinkle on garlic, salt, pepper, and pepper flakes. Next lay on 3 oz. mozzarella, followed by the spinach, tomatoes, and remaining mozzarella. Sprinkle on the Parmesan and Romano, then the ricotta dollops, then place on pizza steel (or stone) and bake for about 12 minutes, turning 90 degrees a couple times as it cooks, until the top of the cheese begins to brown. Remove and allow to sit for several minutes, cut into pieces, and serve.

3. Any additional ingredients can be added including pepperoni or prosciutto as well as other veggies out of the garden.

Spanish Chorizo and Cotija Pizza

We really enjoy the flavor of chorizo in many dishes, as well as cotija cheese which is like Parmesan's cousin, fresh and salty with nice texture. Spanish chorizo sausage is also a great alternative on our Napoli style pizza when pepperoni isn't handy. I may not be going back to pepperoni after enjoying this new flavor profile!

Ingredients

- 12 oz pizza dough, homemade or store bought
- 2 oz Spanish chorizo sliced thin
- 3 oz crumbled Cotija cheese
- 14 oz peeled San Marzano tomatoes lightly crushed (½ can)
- 4 oz mozzarella cheese chopped
- 1 large tomato or 2-3 Roma tomatoes cored and sliced thin
- 1 large jalapeno sliced and cored (optional)
- ½ cup fresh basil
- 1 tbsp good olive oil
- Semolina flour

1. Make the dough or use store bought, about 12 ounces is required for a 13-inch pizza. Roll out the dough, shape to fit the peel, then place on the peel (sprinkled with semolina). Heat oven to 450° F and allow pizza steel (or stone) to heat about 20 minutes (while preparing the pizza).

2. Spread the San Marzano tomatoes around the crust to cover, then add the Spanish Chorizo slices, followed by the tomatoes, jalapenos, then mozzarella, and finally sprinkle the Cotija on. Place on pizza steel (or stone) and bake for about 12 minutes, turning 90 degrees a couple times as it cooks, until the top of the cheese begins to brown.

3. Once browned remove from the oven and allow to sit for several minutes, drizzle on the olive oil and sprinkle on the basil leaves. Cut into pieces and serve.

Carolyn's Skillet Pasta Pie

This is what I call a "travel dish" that Carolyn makes before traveling, it takes some work, but there are leftover meals for days. We use home grown cherry tomatoes for this in the summer. I don't use all the sauce in the pie, but keep some "back" (as Grandma Tate used to say) to wake up each leftover dish. Hot sausage or stick pepperoni can be added to the sauce to bring the dish home! To reheat leftovers, I cut the pie into medium pieces, spoon sauce into a baking dish, and on top, bake at 350 °F for 8 minutes, then serve along with a piece of toasted Italian bread.

Ingredients

Preheat oven to 425 °F.

- 1 medium eggplant, peeled and cut into ½" pieces
- 2 pints of cherry tomatoes
- 8 garlic cloves, minced
- ¼ cup of olive oil
- ½ tsp red pepper flakes
- 2 large eggs
- 14.5 oz. can diced tomatoes
- 28 oz can San Marzano Peeled Tomatoes, crushed
- 15 oz can diced fire roasted tomatoes
- 28 oz can tomato sauce
- 2 tbsp brown sugar
- 1 tbsp molasses
- 8 oz mushrooms, sliced
- 2 large handfuls spinach, roughly chopped
- 2 oz Parmesan cheese, grated
- 2 oz Romano cheese, grated
- 2 heaping tbsp Ricotta
- 2 tbsp capers, chopped
- ½ cup basil
- 1 lb. pasta, spaghetti or Cellentani are recommended
- 1 cup of reserved pasta water

1. Combine eggplant, tomatoes, garlic, olive oil, red pepper flakes and salt in a large cast iron pan. Stir until the eggplant and tomatoes are coated with oil. Place the pan into the preheated oven and roast for 25-35 minutes until the eggplant is cooked and tomatoes burst. Remove from oven and reduce temperature to 400 °F. Cook the pasta according to package directions, reserving one cup of pasta water before draining, put the pasta back in the pot.

2. Combine the San Marzano tomatoes, tomato sauce, diced tomatoes, fire roasted tomatoes, brown sugar, and molasses in a saucepan. Bring the sauce to a boil, lower heat and simmer for 20 minutes. Stir some of the reserved pasta water into the sauce to get a desired consistency, so it's relatively thin. Separate about 1/4 of the sauce and store in container for leftovers.

3. Sauté the spinach and mushrooms in a separate sauté pan for 5 minutes until the spinach is wilted and mushrooms are softened.

4. Whisk the eggs, remaining 3/4 of tomato sauce, Ricotta, 3/4 of the Parmesan and Romano cheeses and the capers, then fold in the mushrooms and spinach.

5. Add all the ingredients into the pasta pot with the drained, cooked pasta and stir to combine.

6. Transfer pasta mixture into cast iron pan and compress with a spatula to smooth out the mixture.

7. Top with remaining cheese and cook in the oven for 30-35 minutes until the top is browned.

8. Let the pasta pie rest for 10 minutes, top with basil, slice and serve.

Oiled Spinach Mushroom Pasta

We really enjoy fresh vegetables in a pasta dish, especially mushrooms, spinach, and cherry tomatoes. I was inspired by Cook's Illustrated "The Fastest Fresh Tomato Sauce" to create something similar. We use capers for some kick, add white balsamic vinegar with the spinach, and of course add pepperoni into the mix! Shaped pasta is best in this dish which is also great for leftovers.

Ingredients

- 1 lb Cellentani or Campanella pasta
- 2 cups cherry tomatoes
- 8 oz fresh baby spinach
- ½ cup olive oil
- 8 oz slice fresh mushrooms
- 3 cloves garlic peeled and minced
- ½ tsp pepper flakes
- 1 tbsp butter
- 1 tsp raw cane sugar
- 1 tbsp white balsamic
- 3 tsp capers
- 2 inches stick pepperoni
- 1.5 oz Parmesan cheese grated
- 1.5 oz Romano cheese grated

1. Cook the pasta per the package directions and reserve 1 cup of pasta water when done, drain and return to the pot.
2. Cut the stick pepperoni into $1/8^{th}$ inch slices and cut each slice in half. Set aside.
3. While the pasta is cooking, in a deep saucepan pour in the olive oil, add the garlic, capers, and stick pepperoni, then allow to heat at medium for about 5 minutes.
4. Next carefully add the tomatoes and mushrooms and allow to cook at medium high for 10 minutes stirring occasionally- many of the tomatoes should remain whole.
5. After 10 minutes turn off the heat and add the butter, pepper flakes, sugar and mix to combine. Pour the mixture into the pot with the pasta and mix well. Next add the spinach and white balsamic and place the cover on top for about 3 minutes. Remove the cover and mix thoroughly until the spinach begins to wilt down, then add the Parmesan and Romano and give a final mix. Place into bowls and serve with grilled Italian or sourdough bread slices.

Leftover Pasta Refresh

Remember the days of dry left-over pasta and sauce, stuck together in a Tupperware container? I used to mix them together in the morning for lunch, then heat it up on my work truck engine! Nowadays I refresh left over pasta by reinvigorating it with sauteed vegetables, cherry tomatoes, marsala wine, and white balsamic vinegar....and garlic bread of course!

Ingredients

- 2 cups left over pasta of any type
- 1 cup cherry tomatoes and/or chopped tomatoes
- 3 handfuls fresh spinach
- 4 oz mushrooms sliced
- 2 cloves garlic minced
- 2 tbsp butter divided
- 4 tbsp olive oil divided
- 2-3 oz hard stick pepperoni sliced in 1/8 pieces (optional)
- 2 tbsp Parmesan grated
- 2 tbsp Romano grated
- 1 tbsp marsala wine
- 1 tsp white balsamic vinegar
- 2 Italian rolls or Italian bread slices

1. In a heated wide deep nonstick pan, add two tablespoons olive oil, 1 tbsp butter, and 1 chopped shallot, allow to sweat some.

2. Peel and slice about 1-2 inches of hard pepperoni, slice into 1/8-inch pieces, cut in half, then add them to the pan for a minute (optional).

3. Next add the mushrooms, allow to cook for a couple minutes, then drop in the tomatoes and cook for another minute, then add the spinach, garlic, and marsala wine, cover and continue to cook. Remove the cover and stir till the spinach just starts to wilt.

4. Add the left-over pasta to the pan, mix to combine and cook for about 8 minutes on medium low heat stirring often. Remove from the pan, spoon into bowls, splash on the balsamic, then top each bowl with Parmesan and Romano cheese.

5. Split an Italian roll, or cut two slices of Italian bread, place them on the grill or large pan sprinkled with remaining olive oil, then heat on medium high till they brown. Serve with the pasta.

Spinach and Mushroom Manicotti

Our version of manicotti, which includes several favorite ingredients such as spinach, mushrooms, San Marzano tomatoes, and Ricotta, is the perfect match of flavors and textures. It's real "comfort food" that is even better as a leftover meal.

1. Cook pasta al dente according to package directions, reserve ¼ cup water, drain and cool on wax paper or a sheet pan with a silicone mat. Preheat the oven to 400 °F.
2. Add olive oil, San Marzano tomatoes, diced tomatoes, tomato sauce, brown sugar, and molasses into a saucepan and simmer on low heat, stirring often, while everything else is being made. Add the reserved pasta water after the pasta has cooked.
3. In a skillet on medium heat, add olive oil, then mushrooms, shallot, salt, and pepper, cook for 3-5 minutes stirring often. Next add the spinach, garlic, and nutmeg to the pan and cook for 1 minute, then remove the pan from heat.
4. In a large bowl, mix ricotta, egg, half of Romano and Parmesan cheese, pepper flakes and the cooked vegetables. Fill the Manicotti shells with the ricotta mixture. Can use a spoon or piping bag.
5. Spread 1-2 tbsp of olive oil on the bottom of a 9" x 13" baking dish then spoon in half of the pasta sauce. Place the filled Manicotti shells in a single layer in the baking dish. It will be tight. Add the remaining pasta sauce and Romano and Parmesan cheese, sprinkle the top with mozzarella cheese.
6. Cover the baking dish and bake for 30 min, (place a sheet pan on a lower rack) then uncover and bake for an additional 5 minutes, until bubbly. Rest for 10 minutes before serving.

Ingredients

- 1 box of Manicotti pasta
- 2 tbsp olive oil
- 8 oz mushrooms chopped
- 1 shallot, chopped
- 1 clove garlic, chopped
- 12 oz spinach chopped
- 12 oz Ricotta cheese
- 1 egg beaten
- ½ cup each Romano/Parmesan
- 1 tsp red pepper flakes
- 4 oz fresh mozzarella, grated
- A pinch of freshly grated nutmeg
- Salt and pepper to taste

Sauce

- 28 oz can San Marzano peeled tomatoes crushed
- 15 oz can fire roasted diced tomatoes
- 15 oz can tomato sauce
- 2 tsp brown sugar
- 1 tbsp molasses
- 4 tbsp olive oil
- ¼ cup reserved pasta water

Summer Pasta Salad

During the heat of Summer, when the tomatoes are plentiful and we don't feel like a lot of cooking, Carolyn will make this pasta salad. This is one of my favorite Summertime dishes since it's super simple, quick to make, stores well, and is great any time of the day. We'll refresh leftovers with white balsamic, salt and pepper, and pair with grilled sourdough– it's perfect!

Ingredients

Meal:

- 1-16 oz box Cellentani, or Tri-colored Rotini pasta, cooked al dente per package directions
- 1 cup cherry or grape tomatoes, halved
- 3 medium carrots, sliced on the bias
- 3 stalks of celery, sliced on the bias
- 2 scallions (green onions), thinly sliced
- 1 red bell pepper, cored, sliced and chopped
- 3-4 radishes, chopped
- 1 jalapeno, cored and chopped
- 1 broccoli florets, chopped
- ¼ cup fresh parsley, chopped

Dressing:

- ½ cup Filippo Berio red wine vinegar (or similar)
- ½ cup good olive oil
- ½ tsp natural sugar
- ¼ tsp pepper flakes
- ½ tsp salt
- ½ tsp freshly ground pepper
- White balsamic

1. Cook the pasta according to the package directions in salted water and drain.
2. Add red wine vinegar, olive oil, sugar, pepper flakes, salt and pepper into a large bowl and whisk until well blended.
3. Add the pasta to the bowl, along with the vegetables, and toss to combine.
4. Add a splash of white balsamic vinegar before serving.

CJs Traveling Lasagna

Whenever Carolyn traveled for work, she'd make a dish that had plenty of leftovers before she left to save me from cooking so much. I almost always ask for her Lasagna, it's got a depth of flavor, some heat, and reheats well (actually its better the next day). Incorporating hot Italian sausage into the sauce, along with mushrooms and spinach, elevates this dish well ...along with a nice piece of garlic bread on the side!

Ingredients

- 1 box lasagna noodles, cooked al dente
- 2 links Italian hot sausage, or 8 oz breakfast sausage or 8 oz ground beef (or any combination of the 3)
- ½ red onion chopped
- 8 oz fresh spinach
- 4 oz mushrooms chopped
- 4 garlic cloves minced
- 1 medium shallot minced
- ¼ cup Marsala wine
- 15 oz Ricotta
- 28 oz can San Marzano Whole Peeled Tomatoes crushed
- 15 oz can diced tomatoes
- 15 oz can of tomato sauce
- 6 tbsp olive oil divided
- 1 tbsp brown sugar
- 1 tbsp molasses
- ¼ tsp fennel seeds (optional)
- 1 egg
- 2 oz Parmesan grated and divided
- 2 oz Romano grated and divided
- Handful of fresh basil
- Salt and pepper to taste.

1. Combine the peeled, crushed, and diced tomatoes, 2 tbsp of olive oil, brown sugar, molasses, and fennel seeds (optional) into a Dutch oven. Bring to a boil then simmer for 30 minutes to an hour. Add enough reserved pasta water to the pasta sauce until you have a desired consistency.

2. Cook the lasagna noodles according to the package directions. Reserve ½ to 1 cup of pasta water before discarding it. Place the drained noodles onto wax paper in a single layer.

3. Cook the sausage and/or ground beef in a separate sauté pan, drop in the onions and cook a few more minutes, then add to the pasta sauce while it's cooking. Preheat the oven to 375 °F

4. Add 2 tbsp of olive oil to the sauté pan, then add the spinach, mushrooms, garlic, and shallot and cook for 2-3 minutes until translucent, then add the Marsala wine and cook for another 2 minutes.

5. In a mixing bowl, combine the egg, ricotta, 1 ½ oz of Parmesan, 1 ½ oz of Romano.

6. Coat the bottom of a 13" by 9" baking dish with remaining olive oil and create the following layers, sauce, lasagna noodles, ricotta mixture, then repeat the sauce, lasagna noodles and ricotta mixture, repeating until the pan has enough height. On the top layer of lasagna noodles, place another layer of sauce, the remaining cheese and torn basil leaves on top.

7. Cover the baking dish with foil, cook for 30-40 minutes covered then 5-10 minutes uncovered until the internal temperature reaches between 165 – 175 °F. I place a cookie sheet on the bottom shelf of the oven to catch any spillage. Let rest for about 10 minutes before cutting and serving.

Catch All Calzones

Whenever we run out of Italian rolls for grinders we make calzones, with leftover deli meats, cheeses, mushrooms, spinach, onions, anything hanging around. This approach allows us to use up these items, so they don't go bad, and get a nice dinner, that's a super easy leftover to reheat and serve later.

Ingredients

- 24 oz fresh pizza dough
- Provolone cheese
- Black forest ham or similar
- Pepperoni
- Hot capicola or similar
- Onions (optional)
- Spinach
- Mushrooms sliced (optional)
- Ricotta
- Basil
- Anything else hanging around
- 28 oz can San Marzano tomatoes crushed
- 28 oz can tomato sauce
- 15 oz can diced fire roasted tomatoes
- 4 tbs olive oil
- 2 tsp molasses
- 2 tsp dark brown sugar
- 3 cloves garlic minced

1. Process the San Marzano tomatoes with a potato masher in a small Dutch oven, pour the cans of tomatoes in, followed by the molasses, brown sugar, olive oil, and garlic, then simmer while making the calzones, stirring occasionally.

2. Drop the dough ball out of the bowl onto a well-floured counter and cut into 6 equal size pieces (use a scale). Roll each piece out to a thickness of about 1/8". Preheat the oven and pizza stone (metal) to 450 °F to allow it to heat for at least 30 minutes.

3. Add the toppings that are available to each calzone, starting with the provolone cheese, spinach, deli meats, vegetables, and finally a tbsp of ricotta. I just make everything as even as possible.

4. Brush the beaten egg on for "glue" and gently fold each calzone into a small "package", then cut 3 slits across the top of each. Place on a peel sprinkled with semolina, then place on the pizza steel and cook for 12- 16 minutes, rotating halfway through (or until they are brown and bubbly).

5. Place a ramekin on each and fill with the sauce mixture for dipping, then place the calzone down and it's done. Save the leftover sauce and calzones for later.

Chicken and Duck

After picking up whole chickens on sale (free range, no chemicals), we make either fried chicken or roasted chicken, depending on the leftover dishes we feel like, or in-house ingredients.

We developed this playbook section to document easy and repeatable ways to utilize both roasted (the majority of the time) and fried chicken, plus it provides us several days worth of meals. I normally make stock to use left-over parts, save money, and so nothing goes to waste.

Roasted Chicken with Cranberry Sauce:

Andreas Viestad is the inspiration behind our roasted chicken. It incorporates starting with high heat, sealing in the juices, then reducing to lower temperature, dropping to 165F. The method allows the skin to crisp, but the meat stays moist and tender.

Another tip is to let the bird warm to room temperature before cooking. Normally we'll have the leg/thigh portion initially, along with noodles, mashed root vegetables, or mushroom bread pudding, and our homemade cranberry sauce (keep a bag in the freezer). The remaining pieces are excellent for pizza, garlic buffalo sandwiches, hand pies, and fajitas.

Ingredients

Chicken:
- 1 large free-range chicken
- Olive oil
- 1 tsp salt
- 1 tsp pepper
- 1 – 2 tsp paprika

Cranberry Sauce:
- 3 cups cranberries (fresh or frozen)
- 1 cup water
- ¼ cup sugar
- ¼ cup honey
- 2 tbsp brandy
- Juice and zest from 1 orange or 2 clementines
- ½ jalapeno finely chopped

1. Pull the bird out of the refrigerator at least an hour before starting and allow it to warm up (adjust based on outside temperature).
2. Unwrap the chicken and rinse out well, removing the innards and any fat. Pat dry then coat well with olive oil then salt and pepper, followed by the Paprika. Preheat the oven to 450 °F.
3. Use the leftover parts and start the stock making process ("Basics" section). Pull out and use any frozen wingtips as well.
4. While the chicken is in the oven, or just prior, make the cranberry sauce by placing all the ingredients in a small saucepan, bring to a boil stirring, then simmer for 10 minutes uncovered (or until about half of the cranberries have "popped", remove from the heat.
5. Place the bird on a grate inside a good size roasting pan and place in the center of the oven with the lid off and roast at 450 °F for about 20 minutes.
6. Reduce the heat to 350 °F and cook for an additional 20-25 minutes with the lid on, then uncover and cook for an additional 20-30 minutes while checking the temperature to get to 165 °F. Once the thicker areas hit temperature remove from the oven and allow to rest for about 15 minutes before carving, garnish with the cranberry sauce.

Chicken Two Ways-Fried

1. We don't have an old Family recipe for fried chicken so we use Emeril Lagasse's "Spicy Buttermilk Fried Chicken" recipe from "Essential Emeril" replacing two cups of the flour with cornmeal.
2. The first leftover dish we make is "Chicken and Waffles", making waffles in our decades old Carousel waffle iron, using either the antique Better Homes and Garden's "New Cookbook" recipe or with Kodiak Cake's mix depending on what's around the house.
3. For the sauce we mix 4 ounces of our homemade peach pepper jelly with 3 tbsp local honey, bring just to a boil, and serve or use 2 oz warmed natural maple syrup and lingonberry jam on top.
4. After this we take a look at the "Chicken Playbook" section and develop our leftover strategy again working to utilize what's available in the house, of course vegetable corn rice or desert dirty rice is always on the menu.

Old Bay Chicken Corn Salad Sandwich

Whenever we have roasted or fried chicken leftovers one of our "go to" dishes are chicken salad sandwiches. Over time we've elevated this version by making celery the star ingredient, using "Old Bay" hot sauce to complement the celery and add depth of flavor, then adding grilled corn.

Ingredients

- 1 leftover chicken breast chopped finely
- 1 large celery stalk split and finely chopped
- ½ medium red pepper sliced and finely chopped
- ⅓ medium onion (or whites from 2 spring or green onions) chopped
- 1 small ear of leftover roasted corn kernels
- 1 medium jalapeno cored and chopped finely
- 2-3 leaves Romaine lettuce cored and cut in large pieces
- 2 tbsp finely chopped fresh sage
- 2-3 tbsp homemade mayonnaise
- 2-3 tsp Old Bay hot sauce
- 3-4 full tsp finely chopped apple
- 4 slices whole grain bread (like Dave's Killer 21 grain)
- 2 tbsp butter
- Cilantro

1. Melt the butter on a griddle and grill both sides of the four pieces of bread and place on plates. I like to grill my bread to give the sandwich a more "deli feel" and not dry out. Distribute the Romaine leaves to cover two pieces.
2. In a medium mixing bowl add the celery, red pepper, onion, corn, jalapeno, chicken, mayonnaise, Old Bay, apple, and sage then mix to combine. Salt and pepper to taste.
3. Using a large spoon distribute the chicken salad evenly between the two slices of bread with lettuce on them, garnish with cilantro, then place the remaining bread on top, cut in half to serve. This is one sandwich that requires a fork!

Quick Chicken Fajitas

After making a roasted or fried chicken there are always some leftovers, and we look for ways to integrate them into easy to prepare dishes. One of my favorite morning meals to make are fajitas, using fresh vegetables (from the garden, if possible) cooked for a short duration to maintain their crisp texture, chipotle sour cream instead of cheese, and then topped off with our homemade barbeque sauce and red wine vinegar tomatoes.

Ingredients

- 6 - 8 oz left over chicken course chopped
- ½ medium onion sliced
- 1 large jalapeno course chopped
- ½ medium red bell pepper course chopped
- 1 cored and chopped large tomato or 2-3 plum/cherry tomatoes halved
- 2 tbsp (heaping) sour cream
- 1 tsp chopped chipotle w/adobo sauce
- 2 tbsp peanut oil
- 2 tbsp red wine vinegar
- 2 tbsp "Johnson's BBQ sauce (or personal favorite)
- 2 large tortillas 10" (burrito Grande)
- 1 tbsp lime juice

1. Mix the sour cream, chipotle, and lime juice together and set aside. Drizzle red wine vinegar over the chopped tomatoes.

2. Heat the tortillas in a flat cast iron pan, turning often, till they just begin to harden up and plate.

3. Heat the oil in a second cast iron pan to about 325 °F drop in the onions, red pepper, and jalapenos. Stir often until the peppers change color and onions soften. Next drop in the chicken, adjust the temp down, and heat up and brown for a couple minutes, salt and pepper to taste, stirring once or twice.

4. Once the chicken has warmed up and while the vegetables are still crisp, stir in the Johnson's barbecue sauce (in the "Basic's Section), mix to combine for about 60 seconds then remove from the heat.

5. Split the chicken mixture between the two tortillas, spoon the sour cream chipotle sauce on top, then cover with the chopped tomatoes, and its done.

Bar-B-Que Chicken Pizza

One of our favorite comfort foods is homemade pizza, so we will use lots of leftovers and fresh vegetables to make all kinds of different variations. Combining leftover roasted chicken, spinach, quick pickled onions, jalapenos, along with our homemade barbeque sauce and fresh ricotta, creates a nice Bar-B-Q Pizza that is easy to make and tastes great.

Ingredients

- 10 oz left over chicken chopped
- 12 oz fresh pizza dough homemade or store bought
- 4 tbsp ricotta cheese
- 3 cloves garlic finely chopped
- ¼ cup organic sugar
- ¼ cup apple cider vinegar
- ½ cup water
- ½ red onion sliced thin
- 1 jalapeno sliced thin, cored
- 4 tbsp Franks hot sauce
- 4 tbsp Johnson's barbeque sauce (or personal favorite)
- 2 large handfuls of spinach
- 3 tbsp olive oil
- Salt and pepper
- Semolina for dusting

1. Place a pizza stone (steel) in the oven, and heat to 450 °F for at least 30 minutes. Whisk together the sugar, apple cider vinegar, and water, mix in the jalapenos and onions, then set aside.
2. While the stone is heating roll out the dough on a floured surface, from the center out, turning often, until it is large enough to fit the peel and stone. Sprinkle semolina on the peel and place the dough on it.
3. Heat up a cast iron pan, and while it's heating brush the crust with olive oil, cover with garlic, lightly salt, and pepper, then add the spinach. Once the pan is about 350 °F add the chicken and brown for several minutes, then add the hot and bar-b-q sauce sauces- stir to coat and remove from the heat, spread around the pizza.
4. Drain and spread the onions and jalapenos around the pizza, followed by dollops of ricotta. Next open the oven and slide the pizza off the peel onto the stone, and cook for about 12-14 minutes turning every four, or until the cheese starts to brown. Remove from the oven and let cool for about 10 minutes then cut and serve. I usually sprinkle on some more good quality olive oil before serving.

Buffalo Blue Cheese Chicken Salad Hoagie

Chicken salad sandwiches are our first choice for leftover fried or roasted chicken. Recently, there were only two wings left over, deep fried with a beautiful crust. It seemed obvious they could be transformed into a chicken salad that had heat from hot sauce, and cool from blue cheese, and of course celery as a star, all together on a garlic roll!

1. Drizzle the olive oil around on a griddle or large pan, sprinkle in the garlic, then lay the rolls in to brown- use a weight and turn 180 degrees at least once. Once they are browned turn them over and allow the outside to heat up. Remove to a plate.

2. In a mixing bowl add the celery, red pepper, onion, jalapeno, chicken and crust pieces, mayonnaise, blue cheese dressing, gorgonzola, hot sauce, barbeque sauce, sage and mix to combine. Taste and add salt and pepper as needed.

3. Lay the lettuce pieces on the rolls, spoon in the chicken salad, sprinkle on the parsley/cilantro, then cut in half and serve.

Ingredients

- 2 leftover fried chicken wings chopped finely (add leg or thigh if needed)
- 2 Italian rolls split
- 2 large celery stalks split and finely chopped
- ½ medium red pepper sliced and finely chopped
- ⅓ medium onion finely chopped
- 1 medium jalapeno cored and chopped finely
- 3-4 leaves Romaine lettuce cored and cut in large pieces
- 2 cloves garlic peeled and minced
- 15-20 parsley and/or cilantro leaves
- 2 tbsp homemade mayonnaise
- 1 tbsp chunky blue cheese dressing
- 1 tbsp crumbled gorgonzola cheese
- 2 tbsp Franks hot sauce
- 1 tbsp Johnson's barbeque sauce
- 5-6 sage leaves
- 2 tbsp olive oil

Buffalo Bar-B-Que Chicken Calzones

Over the last couple years, we have been using our stand mixer to make pizza dough, which we also use for calzones, normally with leftover deli meats, cheeses, mushrooms, spinach, corn, or meats like this roasted chicken. This dish is a play on classic buffalo wings all wrapped up inside a nice crisp dough.

Ingredients

- 10 oz left over chicken
- 24 oz fresh pizza dough
- 2 large handfuls of spinach
- 1 oz aged blue cheese crumbled
- 3 tbsp sour cream
- 1 ear grilled corn kernels removed
- 1 jalapeno sliced
- ½ red onion sliced thin
- 2 stalks celery sliced very thin
- 4 tbsp Franks hot sauce
- 4 tbsp barbeque sauce of choice
- 1-2 eggs beaten
- 1 tbsp unsalted butter
- 3 tbsp peanut oil

1. Drop the doughball onto a well- floured counter or board, roll out and cut into 6 equal size pieces. Roll each piece out to a thickness of about 1/8". Preheat the oven and pizza stone (metal) to 450 °F. Mix the sour cream and blue cheese together and set aside.

2. Heat the peanut oil in cast iron skillet to about 350 °F and drop in the corn and celery, cooking for a few minutes, then add the chicken and allow it to brown for another few minutes stirring often. Next add the Franks, barbeque sauce, and butter to the pan, stir to combine until the butter is melted. Remove from the heat.

3. Spread the spinach evenly across the 6 pieces of dough, add the chicken filling, followed by the onions and jalapenos, then top with the sour cream blue cheese mixture.

4. Fold the sides of each calzone over, using an egg wash to help adhesion, until each one is a nice "packet". Cut three slits on the top of each calzone to allow the steam to escape. Open the oven, place the calzones on the stone, and bake for 12-14 minutes or until browned and bubbly, turning every 4 minutes. Remove and plate along with personal favorite dipping or tomato sauce.

Buffalo Barbeque Chicken Wings

Once we moved out of the city it was hard to get good quality buffalo wings that were made with fresh ingredients, so we started making our own. There are several ways to cook the wings, we prefer to roast them which makes for a real crisp exterior. Why spend the time and money to go out when these are so easy to make at home?

Ingredients

- 8 chicken wings
- 2 tbsp Johnson's Barbecue Sauce
- 3 tbsp melted butter
- 4 tbsp Franks Hot Sauce
- 2 stalks of celery cut in 4-5" strips
- Blue cheese dressing for dipping

1. Preheat the oven to 400 °F.
2. Remove chicken wings tips and save to make chicken stock, they can be frozen to use for this purpose later.
3. Cut the remaining chicken wings in half so you have a drumette and winglets.
4. Place the wings in a roasting pan so they are not touching each other. (We use two glass roasting pans that can fit in the oven side by side.)
5. Cook the wings for about an hour, rotating and flipping them over after 30 minutes. The outside skin should be crispy, and the temperature should be at least 165 °F; we find they taste better at 190-200 °F. Place in a large bowl.
6. Combine the butter, barbeque sauce, and Franks well in a measuring cup, then pour over the wings, and mix to combine.
7. Serve with twice cooked French Fries (Sides Section), celery sticks and blue cheese dressing.

Chicken Corn Okra Rice Hand Pies

Whenever there are leftover ingredients like roasted chicken, rice, grilled corn, and homemade chicken stock available, its fun to make some type of "short" pastry dish, so I decided to try out these chicken and rice hand pies, and included beautiful okra from the refrigerator. We usually serve this with our avocado corn tomato salsa, or homemade chimichurri.

Ingredients

- 2 cups left-over cooked rice
- 12 oz okra sliced
- Kernels off 1 large (or 2 small) grilled corn cobs
- 1 large shallot chopped
- 20 oz puff pastry dough
- 12 oz leftover chicken
- 4 oz chicken stock
- 1 large jalapeno cored and sliced
- ½ large yellow onion sliced
- 1 red bell pepper cored and sliced
- 3 tbsp fresh chorizo
- 4 oz sour cream

1. Preheat the oven to 425 °F, toss the okra with avocado oil. Toast the okra on a sheet tray, turning once, for about 40 minutes. Remove when crispy but not burnt and set aside.
2. Heat the shallots and corn in a deep pan and cook for a few minutes, then add the rice, lower the heat and cover for 8 minutes- stir several times, add stock if required. Once the rice warms up add the okra, mix to combine, then remove from the heat.
3. While the okra is roasting, on a flowered surface, roll the dough into a "log" 10 inches long, then cut into 1" pieces (about 2 oz. each). Roll each piece out until about 1/8".
4. Cook the chorizo in cast iron and once it browns add jalapeno, onion, red pepper and cook till they soften, then add the chicken and cook until it starts to brown, remove from the heat.
5. Spoon one heavy tablespoon of chicken mixture onto each dough disk, top with another heavy tablespoon of okra corn rice, then add one teaspoon stock to each, and finally one teaspoon of sour cream.
6. Adjust the oven to 450 °F, crimp the pies by wetting the inside edges with water, and folding them over, use a fork to "crimp" the entire edge. Use the fork to make several vent holes on each pie, place on a compostable parchment paper lined sheet tray, then place in the oven for about 12-16 minutes (rotating several times) or until golden brown.

Chicken and Duck

The Whole Duck

Holiday season means roasting a whole duck, but I always made it the same way as roasting a chicken- which unfortunately, resulted in much of the duck overcooked and very dry. After watching how some of the "New Scandinavian Cooking" Chefs prepare their ducks, and our philosophy is to not waste anything, I reworked our entire plan for making fresh duck now, so that nothing gets left out and it's more evenly cooked.

Breaking It Down: After finding a chef on YouTube who showed the way to remove all the pieces and use as much as possible, I chose "StellaCulinary.com." Use a laptop to stay consistent, unless you do this frequently. The process keeps the wing top on the breast and leaves the wing tips for stock.

Nothing Goes to Waste: Based on "New Scandinavian Cooking", there are several ways to use the "extra" items, like wingtips, livers, organs, and fat. Most of this is taken care of before, or while, cooking the first duck dish. It also includes rendering the fat from leftover skin or trimmings; making stock from the organs and wingtips; and later making Andreas Viestad's duck liver mousse.

The LOR Duck Playbook: We have several sections of the Playbook, which incorporates our favorite recipes, created by ourselves and others. The methodology makes shopping much easier, especially when things like duck go on sale, since I already know what I need to pick up to create the already documented meals— takes out the guesswork and saves gas. Sometimes we'll come up with something new, and after making it a few times to confirm temperatures and measurements, it becomes part of the playbook. For duck, we use the following recipes:

1. Apple Braised Duck Thighs by Andreas Viestad just can't be beat, it's the first dish we make, super easy and delicious, usually paired with root vegetables or Amish noodles.
2. Juniper Grilled Duck Breast with Cherry Sauce is another easy and tasty meal, great with duck fat potatoes. This recipe is in the "On The Grill" section.
3. Duck Stock is excellent on grilled fish after reducing, simple to make and can be frozen for later.
4. Rendered Duck Fat is super easy to make, stores well, and is my favorite for cooking potatoes and perogies.
5. Andreas Viestad's Duck Liver Mousse is perfect with grilled plums on grilled rye toast. I usually have some beet pickled eggs on the side!

Apple Marinated Duck Thighs (Andreas Viestad S08 US S02 – E06) usually with mashed roots and homemade cranberry or cherry sauce!

Duck Liver Mousse (Andreas Viestad S08 US S02 – E06) with marinated grilled plums and grilled rye toast, perfect with beet pickled eggs and cottage cheese!

Rendered Duck Fat

Our food philosophy is to use everything we can and not waste anything unnecessarily. When I break down a duck every part gets used, including the skin and fat trimmings, which are cooked down and stored for future use in "Duck Fat Potatoes" and other dishes, and lasts for a long time in the refrigerator.

Ingredients

- Duck skin, fat and trimmings from one duck

1. Place the skin and fat trimmings into a cast iron pan and heat at medium until everything is crispy and the fat has all come out as liquid. It helps to use a weight to get even heating on the bigger pieces.

2. Remove the crisp pieces of skin from the pan and discard, then drain the liquid through a small sieve into a mason jar. Place the lid on and store in the refrigerator until needed.

Runner and His Mom

Sides

Momma Deer and Her Twins

Edna's Fermented Cabbage

Years ago, my Aunt Edna and Uncle Pap were visiting and she made Saur kraut in the frying pan mixed with chopped onions. Based on that experience we now use our homemade fermented cabbage, along with red onion and jalapenos for some kick. Great on Reubens, brats, or as a nice side by itself.

Ingredients

Fermented Cabbage:

- 1 head of green cabbage (2-2.5 lbs.)
- 3.5-5 tsp kosher salt (based on taste)
- This will fill two Mason jars

Edna's Saur Kraut:

- 10 oz fermented cabbage
- 4 tbsp tsp red onion chopped
- 2 tbsp jalapeno or similar chiles
- 1 –2 tbsp olive oil. (For two servings)

1. Remove the outer leaves from the head, then thinly slice/chop the cabbage. Place the sliced/chopped cabbage in a metal bowl and sprinkle the salt on. Thoroughly mix the two ingredients and let rest for about an hour.

2. Spoon the cabbage/salt mixture into clean/sterilized 32 oz Mason jars (I sterilize them in the oven at 220 °F for 10 minutes and allow them to cool). We use the compression spring lids to keep everything from floating up, and they have a vent for the gasses.

3. Place these jars into a cool dry place and check in two to three days to vent pressure then reseal, move to the refrigerator, and let stand for at least two weeks. If cabbage is exposed in the jars add brine solution (1 tsp salt per cup water) to recover.

Edna's Fermented Cabbage Kraut

1. Using tongs place the cabbage into a wide nonstick pan in a thin layer, leave the center open and drop the onions and jalapenos there, then cover them with the olive oil. Allow to cook for about 3-5 minutes on medium heat.

2. Once the cabbage starts to dry out stir everything together, then cook another 3-5 minutes, stirring often, until the vegetables just start to soften, and the cabbage may begin to brown slightly. Remove from the heat and serve.

BJ's Duck Fat Potatoes

I've always been a big fan of "home fries", with their sweet cooked onions and a paprika kick, since they go with anything, anytime. I use our rendered duck fat, along with jalapenos, Old Bay seasoning, and rosemary in the background for these, which are great for breakfast or dinner, even in tacos!

Ingredients

- 3 large Yukon Gold potatoes peeled and sliced 3/16-1/4 inch (or cubed)
- 1 large jalapeno cored and chopped
- ½ red pepper chopped
- ½ yellow onion chopped
- 2-3 tbsp duck fat
- ½ tsp Old Bay seasoning
- 2 sprigs rosemary
- ½ tsp salt
- ½ tsp pepper

1. Place the potatoes in salted water in a large bowl for about 10 minutes, mixing around in the water, then drain and pat dry with a towel-we don't want water going into the hot fat! For dinner items like duck or steak I slice them, for breakfast or tacos I use cubes, it's a personal preference.

2. Add 2 tbsp duck fat into a wide nonstick pan, allow to melt, then add 2 sprigs of rosemary, and allow that to cook until the fat reaches a temperature of 350-375 °F.

3. Pull the rosemary out and add the potatoes, then cook at medium until they start to brown, turn and continue cooking till they slightly soften, turning often.

4. Once the potatoes are browned move them to the outside of the pan and add the onions, red pepper, and jalapeno, some salt and pepper and allow to cook another 4-5 minutes, moving them around a couple times. Once the vegetables are translucent add the Old Bay and mix everything together. Recheck for salt, pepper, and Old Bay before serving.

Kathryn's Baked Beans

"Mamaw" Johnson (Kathryn) in Louisiana spent a lot of time cooking and making awesome dishes. She taught me to add simple ingredients into dishes, that provide added depth and a "pop". Whenever we make these beans, and many other dishes, I see us working together in her New Iberia kitchen and it feels nice!

Ingredients

- 16 oz canned baked beans
- 4 tbsp finely chopped onion
- 2 tbsp finely chopped jalapeno or similar chili
- 1 tsp dark brown sugar
- 1 tsp molasses
- 1.5 tbsp apple cider vinegar

1. In a medium saucepan combine all the ingredients and mix well. Bring to a slow boil stirring often, then simmer for about 6 minutes uncovered, until reduced. The vegetables should still be crisp with only a slight change in color.

Roasted Okra

Okra is a vegetable that people either love or hate. After trying it many ways over the years, we found that simple roasting works well for our cooking playbook-it's perfect in vegetable corn rice, which we eat a lot of, tastes like candy to me, and is super easy to make.

Ingredients

- 2 cups fresh okra
- 2 tbsp peanut oil
- ½ tsp salt
- ½ tsp pepper

1. Rinse the okra, pat dry then remove the tops and bottoms. Cut each piece into 3/8"-1/2" sections. Set the oven to 400 °F.

2. Place the okra in a plastic bag or bowl, pour in the peanut oil, and add the salt and pepper. Mix around till all the pieces are well covered.

3. Place the okra pieces on a sheet pan (lined with a silicone baking mat) and spread around so they are not touching.

4. Place the pan in the middle of the oven and roast for about 25 minutes, turning once midway through. The ends should show some color when they are done, then remove and allow to cool down, ready for use.

CJ's Avocado Corn Salsa

Our inspiration for this recipe started as a topping for southwestern spiced grilled steak, but it also goes with empanadas, or other Southwest dishes, where a fresh citrus like salsa can add some brightness. Great way to use left-over grilled corn and fresh vegetables out of the garden or from the store.

Ingredients

- 1 large or 2 small ears left over roasted corn- kernels removed
- 1-2 small-medium avocados sliced and chopped
- 1 large or 2 medium tomatoes cored and chopped
- 1 large jalapeno cored and chopped
- ½ red pepper chopped
- 1 lime juiced
- 2 green onions chopped
- 2 tbsp apple cider vinegar
- 2 tbsp olive oil
- 1 small handful of cilantro
- Salt and pepper

1. After slicing the avocado, mix with the lime juice and set aside. In a large bowl combine the corn, avocado, tomato, jalapeno, red pepper, green onions, apple cider vinegar, and olive oil.

2. Once combined gently mix in the avocado, then salt and pepper to taste. Adjust the vinegar level, if necessary, then plate and add cilantro to garnish.

Desert Dirty Rice

Rice dishes are a great inexpensive side dish option with multiple variations. My favorite is combining corn, pinto beans, and Tabasco chipotle hot sauce, with Jasmine vegetable rice. This combination creates a whole different experience and depth of flavor. This is excellent with a good steak or pork chop, and homemade barbeque sauce, for a real Southwest feel!

Ingredients

- 4 cups cooked jasmine rice (cooked with half water and remainder vegetable stock)
- 15 oz corn (cut off grilled or canned)
- ½ cup vegetable stock
- 15 oz pinto beans drained
- ½ red pepper cored and chopped
- 1 shallot finely chopped
- 1 jalapeno cored and chopped
- 1 tsp Tabasco Chipotle hot sauce
- 1 tbsp butter
- 1 tbsp white wine
- 2 tbsp oil
- 1-2 tsp white balsamic vinegar
- 8 oz roasted okra (optional)

1. Cook rice with ½ water and ½ vegetable stock per directions. Set it aside.

2. Sweat vegetables in 2 tbsp oil (about 4-5 minutes) then add the wine and allow to cook off for a minute, followed by the hot sauce and then mix to combine.

3. Next add one tbsp butter along with corn and pinto beans, mix and heat for a couple minutes (back to a boil), then add the rice and mix well, adding up to ½ cup stock slowly if necessary. Finally add the roasted okra if desired. Salt and pepper to taste.

4. Sprinkle on the white balsamic and mix just prior to serving.

Ginger Rice

Whenever I find okra in the supermarket my mind immediately goes to Ginger rice, which includes roasted corn as well. I like make enough for several meals since it's a great leftover. This goes well with coconut shrimp, or our ultimate favorite seared tuna loin!

Ingredients

- 3 cups cooked Jasmine Rice
- 12 oz roasted okra
- 2 green onions chopped
- ½ medium red pepper chopped
- 3 cloves garlic minced
- ¾ cup veg stock
- 2 tbsp peanut oil
- 1 ear roasted corn off the cob
- 1 large shallot chopped
- 1 medium jalapeno cored and chopped
- 2-3 tbsp grated fresh ginger
- 1 tsp gochujang
- ½ tsp sesame oil
- ½ tsp tamari soy
- ½ tsp mirin
- 2 tbsp sake
- ½ tsp pepper flakes
- ½ tsp rice wine vinegar
- Sesame seeds

1. In a deep pan add the oil, corn, shallot, jalapeno, and red pepper, then allow to sweat a few minutes, next add the sake, cook another minute, then add the veg stock, gochujang, soy, sesame oil, mirin, garlic, and pepper flakes and stir to combine. Allow to reduce approximately 25% stirring often.

2. Once the broth has reduced add in the rice, then roasted okra, stir to combine and heat until the broth is absorbed, then add the ginger and mix to combine. Remove from the heat.

3. Add a splash of rice wine vinegar just before serving and garnish with green onions and sesame seeds.

Sides

Vegetable Corn Rice

One of our favorite side dishes is rice- it's the perfect ingredient for incorporating different flavors and textures, its relatively inexpensive, and can be used for any meal, and pretty much any protein. We started incorporating some of our grilled and roasted vegetables and fruits into it and over time developed a base recipe that allows for all kinds of free forming!

Ingredients

- 3 cups left-over or cooked jasmine rice
- 2 leftover grilled corn kernels off the cob
- 1 large shallot chopped
- ½ red pepper chopped
- 1 jalapeno cored and chopped
- 2 tbsp marsala wine
- ½ tsp Tabasco Chipotle hot sauce
- ½ cup vegetable stock
- 2 tbsp avocado or peanut oil
- 2 tbsp unsalted butter
- Roasted okra (optional)
- Grilled pineapple (optional)

1. Add the oil to a deep nonstick or stainless pan, then add the shallots, jalapeno, red pepper, and corn then cook for a few minutes. Next add the marsala wine and allow to cook off for a couple minutes, then add the stock (warm works best), hot sauce, and bring to a quick boil. Drop in the rice and mix it up well, then lower the heat and cover for about 8 minutes, stirring every couple minutes.

2. Add more stock if required. Once the rice warms up add the butter and mix really well, then salt and pepper to taste. Remove from the heat and mix in any cooked vegetables or fruits, mix well, then plate and serve.

3. We typically will add roasted okra, and/or grilled pineapple depending on the protein that's being made and will incorporate almost anything from the garden like string beans, lima beans, shishitos, peas, whatever is available.

Honey Chipotle Apples and Onions

Pickled apples and onions are an excellent condiment that can change the taste of many sandwiches, and is a great alternative to store bought items. While preparing a left-over barbeque rib sandwich I included chipotle, mustard, and local honey. It's a great blend of flavors that goes well with pork, chicken, or ham, also good on pizza!

Ingredients

- 1 medium red onion peeled and sliced
- 1 medium apple peeled, cored, and sliced
- 2 tsp crushed chipotle with adobo sauce
- 2 tsp Dijon mustard
- 4 tsp local honey
- ½ cup apple cider vinegar
- 1 large jalapeno cored and chopped crossways
- ½ cup apple juice
- 1 tbsp butter

1. In a small saucepan combine the onion, apple, jalapeno, mustard, apple cider vinegar, apple juice, honey, and chipotle. Mix well to combine, bring to a boil, then allow to simmer for about 12 minutes, until it reduces by about 40%.

2. Next add the butter and mix, then add salt and pepper to taste. Remove from heat and serve or transfer to mason jar and store in the refrigerator for later.

3. Left over grilled plums can be added to this and works well if they are available.

Western Mushy Peas

Carolyn has been making Fish and Chips at home for a while now, and we have seen several English chefs that like to include "mushy peas" with it. When I first tried making and tasting them, I have to say the dish was kind of timid, so I took a shot at livening it up a bit to get closer to our taste. It's a really easy and delicious dish that is also good for leftovers.

Ingredients

- 16 oz frozen organic peas
- ½ tsp salt
- ¼ cup heavy cream
- ½ tsp pepper
- 2 oz diced pancetta cubed
- 1 shallot finely chopped
- 1 clove garlic finely chopped
- 1 jalapeno cored and chopped
- 1 tbsp butter
- 1 tbsp peanut or avocado oil
- Cilantro

1. Sprinkle the oil into a cast iron or nonstick skillet, then drop in the pancetta and allow to cook down for about 2 minutes.

2. Next add the frozen peas, salt, and pepper and cook for 3-4 minutes more (raise the heat if necessary), then add the shallots, jalapeno, heavy cream, and garlic then cook until the cream reduces a bit.

3. Use a potato masher to "mush" the peas (not too much), then add the tbsp of butter and combine softly, sprinkle on fresh cilantro to finish.

Nordic Root Vegetable Mash

For years we made mashed potatoes and used them for leftovers like the potato pancakes Grandma Tate would make in her Philly rowhouse kitchen. Since then, New Scandinavian cooking has heavily influenced our thinking on food, and particularly the use of root vegetables in side-dishes like this, which are excellent as leftovers, have more flavor than plain potatoes, and go with many types of protein!

Ingredients

- 1 large swede (rutabaga) peeled
- ½ celery root peeled
- 2 parsnips peeled
- 3 large Yukon gold potatoes peeled
- 2-3 yellow beets peeled
- 2 large rosemary sprigs
- ¼ tsp nutmeg
- 3 tbsp butter
- 3 tbsp sour cream
- ¼ cup half and half
- 2 tbsp grated horseradish
- ½ leek finely chopped parsley
- 1 tsp salt
- ½ tsp pepper
- Any combination of local root vegetables can be used

1. In a large pot bring approximately 8 cups of water to a boil (include one tsp of salt, and rosemary sprigs). While the water is heating peel and slice/chop the root vegetables coarsely and place in the boiling water in this order-swede and celery root first, five minutes later the parsnips and beets, 15 minutes later the potatoes and leek. Allow this to boil covered until the vegetables start to float and are al dente then pull from the heat and drain.
2. Place the vegetables back in the pot (remove the rosemary sprigs) and add butter, sour cream, half and half, horseradish, salt, pepper, nutmeg and combine with hand masher. Adjust addition of butter and sour cream to get a firm consistency, check for salt and pepper. Add fresh parsley or sauteed beet greens leaves as garnish when serving.
3. Leftovers can be placed in a baking dish, covered with panko breadcrumbs, corn meal, grated Parmesan, Romano cheese, and Old Bay seasoning, heated in a 350 °F oven for about 10 minutes, then under a "high" broiler until the top just starts to brown, is great with seafood.

Bobbi's Spinach and Pea Risotto

Risotto is one of those dishes that is great with proteins or by itself, but if not done properly can end up too mushy or too crunchy. Carolyn uses hot vegetable stock and adds it slowly, which requires a lot of focus and oversight, but the results are worth it every time, and who doesn't love peas and spinach!

Ingredients

- 2 tbsp olive oil
- 2 tbsp butter
- 1 large shallot, minced
- ½ cup white wine
- 1 cup Arborio rice
- 4 cups of vegetable stock, hot
- 1 cup thawed frozen or fresh peas
- 4 oz spinach, roughly chopped
- 1 oz Romano cheese, grated
- 1 oz Parmesan cheese, grated
- Salt and pepper

1. In a large sauté pan, heat oil and butter over medium heat for about 1 minute.
2. Add shallots and sauté them for about 2 minutes until they are softened.
3. Stir in rice and cook for about 2 minutes, stirring constantly.
4. Add wine and cook until all the wine is absorbed, about 2 minutes.
5. Add 1 cup of hot broth to the pan and stir constantly until most of the broth is absorbed.
6. Continue to add broth, one ladle at a time, stirring constantly until the broth is absorbed before adding more broth.
7. Continue adding broth until the rice is cooked to "al dente".
8. Add the peas, spinach, and cheese then stir to combine until spinach is wilted.
9. Add salt and pepper to taste and serve warm.

Grilled Baked Potato

Every once in a while, we get the urge to have an old-fashioned baked potato and a nice grilled steak—a classic combination. Using the microwave to cook them almost completely ensures the centers are finished, and then use the grill to crisp up the skin and add flavor, which saves both time and gas.

Ingredients

- 1 russet potato scrubbed and dried
- 1 tbsp olive oil
- 1 tbsp freshly grated horseradish root
- 1 tbsp butter (optional)
- 2 tbsp sour cream
- Salt and pepper to taste
- Chopped chives

1. Pierce the potato on all sides with a fork to allow the steam to escape while cooking.
2. Cook potato in the microwave for about 5-7 minutes at "Potato" setting, on a microwave safe plate.
3. Remove the hot potato with tongs and place it on enough foil to wrap it completely (approximately 12" x 16").
4. Drizzle olive oil on potato, then add salt and pepper.
5. Wrap it up so the foil edges are on top and fold to create a "handle".
6. Place on a hot grill preheated to 450 °F and cook for 15-20 minutes, turning once or twice, then remove.
7. Unwrap foil, place potato on dinner plate, and immediately cut longwise about two thirds deep, then carefully push the ends of the cut together to open the potato.
8. Add horseradish, butter (optional), sour cream, (salt and pepper to taste) to the opening and enjoy. Chopped chives are another great addition to these.
9. For each potato made increase the other ingredients proportionally.

Sides

Russet and Sweet Potato Fries

French fries are a popular side dish around the world. In our search for the best homemade fries, we finally found that making our own, out of fresh local or homegrown Russet and sweet potatoes, always turned out the best. Mixing the two types together creates a nice flavor blend as well with hot wings!

Ingredients

- 1 Russet potato
- 1 white yam/sweet potato without curves (as straight as possible)
- Enough peanut oil to cover fries when cooking, about 1 ½ to 2 inches deep
- Salt and pepper

1. Cut the fries into ¼-by-¼ inch fries by cutting ¼" slabs an then cutting them into ¼" strips. Fries should be about 4" long. If the fries are too long, they can be cut in half.
2. Next place the fries into a bowl filled with water and soak for 15-30 minutes.
3. Preheat oil to 375 °F. I use an electric deep fryer with a basket.
4. Drain the fries and dry them completely in between two kitchen towels before putting them in the fryer. This is very important.
5. Prepare a draining rack by placing paper towels on a cookie sheet and put the cooking rack on top of the paper towels.
6. Cook the French fries twice.
    - **First Cook -** Carefully drop the fries into the oil until they just start to brown, about 10 - 20 minutes depending on the thickness of the fry and the type of potato. The sweet potato/yam fries will take about twice as long as the Russet potato to cook so I cook each type of potato in separate small batches.
        - Remove fries from oil and drain on the prepared draining rack.
        - Repeat until all fries have been cooked once.
    - **Second Cook -** In small batches, drop fries in oil and cook for 30-60 seconds until they are browned.
        - Drain on the prepared rack.
        - Salt and pepper to taste while the fries are still hot.
7. Serve with your favorite dipping sauce, we like to use our homemade barbecue sauce.

Japanese Cucumber Salad

We wanted a cucumber salad at home similar to the ones we get in sushi restaurants, but with our taste profiles. We tried to replicate the flavors made by our sushi Master from Bel Air, MD (pronounced Blair) that adds a nice touch with homemade or supermarket sushi.

Ingredients

- 1 cucumber
- 3 tbsp rice vinegar
- 1 tbsp granulated sugar
- 1 tsp soy sauce (Tamari)
- ½ tsp gochujang
- 1 tbsp of light oil (peanut or avocado)
- 1 tsp Sake
- 1 tsp Mirin
- 3-4 drops of sesame oil
- ¼ jalapeno, finely chopped
- ¼ tsp sesame seeds
- ⅛ tsp white pepper

1. Combine the rice vinegar, sugar, soy sauce, gochujang, oil, sesame oil, Sake, mirin, and white pepper into a small bowl and mix well until the sugar is dissolved.
2. Peel the cucumber, cut it in half longways and remove the seeds, then thinly slice, or cut into matchsticks.
3. Add the cucumber and jalapeno to the bowl and mix well.
4. Sprinkle sesame seeds on top when serving.

Garden Vegetable Orzo

In our constant search to use leftover vegetables, we most often use rice, however some dishes are much better with orzo. Carolyn's made many variations, my favorite is green beans and/or asparagus, and of course roasted okra. The dish comes together quickly, is inexpensive, and helps clear out the refrigerator so nothing goes to waste. The leftovers refresh well, with our favorite use being with some pork roll for breakfast!

Ingredients

- 8 oz orzo (½ box cook according to directions on the box)
- ¼ cup reserved water used to cook the pasta
- 1 shallot chopped
- 1 shucked ear of corn or an 11 oz can of corn
- 6 oz cherry tomatoes cut in half
- 1 jalapeno chopped
- ½ red pepper, chopped
- Asparagus or green beans cut in 2" pieces
- Roasted okra cut in 1" pieces or zucchini (optional) chopped
- 6 oz mushrooms, chopped
- 8 oz spinach or kale (optional), roughly chopped
- 1 tbsp butter
- 1 tbsp olive oi
- 1 tsp hot sauce
- ¼ cup vegetable stock
- ¼ cup wine or Sake
- White balsamic (or other acid)

1. Cook orzo according to the package directions, reserve ¼ cup pasta water.
2. In a nonstick sauté pan, heat oil and butter over medium heat for about 1 minute, then sauté the vegetables for about 2 minutes, until they just start to soften.
3. Add the wine (Marsala, white wine, or Sake) and cook for 3 minutes to cook off the alcohol.
4. Add the pasta, stock, reserved pasta water and hot sauce, then simmer for an additional 5 minutes.
5. Add butter, and acid (lemon, lime, white balsamic vinegar, rice vinegar).
6. Salt and pepper to taste and serve.

Barbeque Fried Brussels

Our favorite lunch at the Phoenix airport was a Brussel sprout salad, then I started eating them fried at the "Palace Hotel and Restaurant" in Prescott. We enjoyed them so much that we started making them at home. They are an excellent side for chorizo burgers— plus the peanut oil can be filtered and reused which saves money!

Ingredients

- 8 oz Brussel sprouts cut in half
- 1 tbsp Johnson's barbecue sauce (or personal choice)
- Peanut oil
- Salt and pepper

1. Fill the deep fryer with enough peanut oil to cover the sprouts. Once the deep fryer reaches 350 °F, place the sprouts in a basket and then into the oil. Cook them for about 4-6 minutes (or until they start to brown), pull out and drain on a paper towel. Place in a large bowl, add the barbeque sauce, then mix the sprouts to coat, add salt and pepper to taste.

2. We've tried canola and other oils, but the taste of peanut oil is perfect with these, so I don't use an air fryer either. The peanut oil can be saved and reused later for more sprouts, fries, or egg rolls.

Braised Green Beans

Who doesn't love fresh green beans, especially when they are nice and tender. Back in the day folks would boil them until they were ready to fall apart- what a shame. We like to braise ours in home-made vegetable stock and a hit of white wine, along with pancetta for some spice and texture. These are great alone as a side, but we really like using them in vegetable corn rice or vegetable orzo.

Ingredients

- 8 – 10 oz green beans, trimmed
- 1 tbsp butter
- 2 tbsp olive oil
- 1 shallot, chopped
- ¼ cup white wine
- 1 cup vegetable stock
- 2 oz pancetta
- Toasted sliced almonds
- Salt and freshly ground pepper to taste

1. In a small sauté pan add the pancetta and heat until cooked through, about 10 minutes. Set it aside.

2. Melt the butter with olive oil in a medium sauté pan over medium heat, then add shallots and cook for 2 minutes until shallots are softened.

3. Next add the green beans and stock, then sauté on medium-low heat for 20 minutes.

4. Add wine and cook for an additional 5 minutes, until the liquid is cooked off, to brown the beans.

5. Mix the pancetta into the beans, add salt and pepper to taste, then top with sliced almonds and serve.

The beans can be cut into 2-inch pieces and stirred into vegetable rice or orzo.

Carolyn's Creamed Spinach

One of the ingredients we always have in the refrigerator is spinach. It goes on anything including burgers, pizza, manicotti ... the list goes on. However, when we feel like going back to "meat and potatoes" Carolyn's creamed spinach is the perfect side, real comfort food and its quick, easy to prepare, and delicious.

Ingredients

- 20 oz fresh spinach, roughly cut
- 1 shallot, chopped
- 2 tbsp butter
- ⅓ cup cream (or half and half)
- Pinch of freshly grated nutmeg
- ⅛ tsp pepper flakes
- Salt and pepper to taste

1. Melt the butter in a large saucepan over medium heat.
2. Add the shallots and cook them until they are softened (about one minute).
3. Stir in the cream and bring the mixture to a boil, then cook for 1-2 minutes.
4. Add the spinach and cook for another 2 minutes, stirring often.
5. Add the nutmeg, pepper flakes, salt and pepper and stir to combine, then ready to serve.

Drew's Roasted Carrots

Simple vegetable side dishes can be elevated with very little work and still maintain their flavor, color, and texture. Many years ago, one of my friends from work (initials D.B) made this carrot dish as part of a quick dinner before we headed to the plant, it was simple and delicious, so it's been in my playbook ever since.

Ingredients

- 4 - 6 carrots peeled and halved longwise
- Karo Syrup
- 1-2 tbsp butter cubed
- ½ tsp cayenne or red pepper flakes
- ½ tsp cardamom
- Splash of white balsamic vinegar
- Salt and pepper to taste

1. Preheat oven to 400 °F.
2. Place carrots in a single layer in a 2 QT baking dish.
3. Sprinkle spices and cubed butter on top of the carrots, and then pour enough Karo Syrup in the dish to cover the carrots halfway.
4. Cook for 20-30 minutes, turning once, until carrots are tender.
5. Sprinkle white balsamic vinegar on top of the carrots before serving.

Coconut Rice

We make several different vegetable Jasmine rice dishes, usually based on the protein, (except for sushi rice sticks). Seared tuna, or seared garlic shrimp, are perfect with this dish. The rice can be cooked in milk, but I add it later to make it creamier. Left over grilled pineapple provides a nice depth of flavor and additional texture when added.

Ingredients

- 1 cup jasmine rice
- 1.5 cups water
- 1 tbsp Sake
- 1 shallot finely chopped
- 1 jalapeno cored and finely chopped
- 1 tsp fresh grated ginger
- 4-6 oz coconut milk
- Cilantro
- Grilled pineapple (optional)
- Roasted okra (optional)

1. Combine the rice, water, and Sake and cook per package directions.

2. Once the rice is done add the shallot, ginger, jalapeno, and coconut milk then heat on low heat and simmer until the milk is absorbed (about 8-10 minutes). Remove from the heat and mix well. If roasted okra or grilled pineapple are available add it in now.

3. Garnish with cilantro.

Classic Diner Home Fries

In all the diners I've eaten in around the country, from the Mayfair Diner in Northeast Philadelphia to Gabby's Restaurant here in Chino Valley Arizona, the one consistent dish they all make is home fries. Its something that is basic and simple, yet for some reason really warms the soul, total comfort food.

Ingredients

- 2 large Yukon Gold potatoes, peeled
- 3-4 tbsp avocado oil
- ½ medium onion chopped
- ½ tsp Icelandic sea salt
- ½ tsp fresh ground pepper
- ½ tsp smoked paprika
- 1 tbsp kosher salt
- 1 small jalapeno chopped (optional)
- Salt and pepper to taste

1. Fill a medium bowl with warm water and add the Kosher salt, mix well. Slice the potatoes about 3/8" thick, longways then again cross ways to make cubes, place in the bowl and stir, allow to sit about 15 minutes, then drain and dry on a kitchen towel.
2. Heat the avocado oil in a wide non stick pan to around 325 °F, then carefully drop in the potatoes and cook for about 8 minutes. Until browned.
3. Turn the potatoes over with the back of a spatula, drop in the onions (and jalapenos) and add the salt and pepper. Continue to cook about 2 minutes, then sprinkle in the paprika and mix well. Test the potatoes for doneness and browning for a couple more minutes. Turn off the heat and plate.
4. These are awesome as a base for creamed chip beef (SOS).

Desserts

JB's Rice Pudding

I always enjoyed eating the rice pudding Grandma Tate made when I was a kid, unfortunately, her recipe was never passed down. After seeing an 18th century "Poor Man's Rice Pudding" from Amelia Simmons "American Cookery", which doesn't use a double boiler, I decided to give it a try with the flavors and local ingredients we like.

Ingredients

- 4 oz jasmine rice uncooked
- 1 qt whole milk
- 1 tbsp unsalted butter cut in cubes
- ¼ tsp nutmeg
- ¼ cup local honey
- ¼ tsp cayenne
- 3 dates chopped
- 1 egg beaten (stirred in while cold)
- 2 tbsp Jim Beam whiskey
- 1 tbsp pine nuts (chopped hazel nuts can be substituted)
- Pinch salt

1. Preheat oven to 325 °F. While the oven heats up mix together all the ingredients in a 2-3 qt. casserole and bring to a boil on the stove, stirring often, then turn off the heat.
2. Place the cover on the casserole and place it in the oven. Stir every 15-20 minutes and watch for the texture to change. This can be removed from the oven anywhere between 45 and 75 minutes based on personal preference of thickness.
3. Spoon onto plates and top with homemade whipped cream.
4. The recipe can be doubled for more servings as required.

Cherry-Vanilla Clafoutis

Once we started raising chickens and ducks we had droves of eggs. Our duck eggs are perfect for baking since they are really rich and go great in this dish which is inspired by Food & Wine's July 2018 edition of a dessert baked in cast iron, that incorporates the cherries from our new trees!

Ingredients

- 2 tbsp unsalted butter
- 5 large eggs (mix chicken and duck eggs)
- ¾ cup granulated sugar
- ¾ cup half and half
- ¼ cup plus 2 tbsp whole wheat flour
- 1 tsp vanilla extract
- 1 tsp lemon zest
- ½ tsp kosher salt
- 8 oz fresh cherries pitted
- ¼-½ cup chopped walnuts or pecans (personal preference)
- Powdered sugar for dusting

1. Preheat the oven to 350° F. Place butter in a 12" cast iron skillet and heat it in the oven until butter is melted, about 10 minutes.
2. Combine eggs, granulated sugar, half and half, flour, vanilla, lemon zest, and salt in a blender until very smooth. Pour batter into a hot skillet and immediately arrange cherries and nuts on top.
3. Bake until the custard is set, about 30 to 35 minutes.
4. Remove from the oven and rest for 15 minutes.
5. Dust with powdered sugar and serve immediately.

Bourbon Grilled Peaches

The smoky flavor of grilled fresh fruit like peaches, plums, pears, and pineapple adds variety to any meal. For peaches from our trees, we've developed a marinate that supports their natural taste and adds some depth, making it perfect on top of French toast, or our favorite with grilled jalapeno biscuits topped with homemade whipped cream!

Ingredients

- 4 peaches seed removed, halved, and sliced (plums or pears too)
- 1 tbsp good quality bourbon
- 2 tsp fermented pepper hot sauce (not vinegar based- optional)
- 1 tbsp dark brown sugar
- ½ tsp cayenne pepper
- 2 tbsp avocado oil
- 1 tbsp butter
- ¼ tsp salt
- ¼ tsp pepper

1. Combine all the ingredients except the peaches into a large zip lock bag and mix very well.
2. Add the peaches to the marinate and mix together by kneading and turning over several times. Allow to rest 30-60 minutes turning a couple more times.
3. Place the peach slices in a cast iron pan with melted butter on the grill's grate at about 400 °F for 3 or 4 minutes, then turn over and cook for another 3-4 minutes or until softened some. Pull from the grill, remove to a dish, salt and pepper to taste then serve.
4. These can be reheated from the refrigerator on the griddle with a tablespoon of butter.
5. We combine these with homemade jalapeno biscuits, halved and grilled, and top with homemade whipped cream for a fantastic dessert.

Candied Pecans and Peanuts

One of the things we like to eat as a snack or desert is nuts, like pecans or peanuts, since they are not filling and taste great. Carolyn started integrating both, along with several sweet ingredients that result in an excellent mix of flavors and textures, which is simple to make and stores well. The only problem is that they are hard to keep around because we can't stop eating them!

Ingredients

- ½ cup brown sugar
- ¼ tsp Kosher salt
- ¼ tsp cinnamon
- 1 tbsp butter
- ¼ tsp vanilla extract
- 2 tbsp water
- 1 cup pecan halves
- ½ cup lightly salted peanuts

1. Add all the ingredients, except the pecans and nuts, into a large shallow pan.
2. Heat the pan over medium heat, continuously stirring the ingredients to combine, then bring to a boil for 4-5 minutes. Be careful not to burn the mixture.
3. Next add the nuts and mix well to combine, then remove from the heat.
4. Preheat oven to 250 °F and line a cookie sheet with silicone or parchment paper.
5. Remove pan from the heat and spoon the nut mixture, using a spatula, onto the cookie- sheet being careful not to touch the mixture or taste it- the heated mixture is very hot.
6. Bake in oven for 20 minutes then remove from the oven and place on a rack to cool. Let the nut mixture cool completely before breaking it up to serve. Can be stored in an airtight container for several weeks.

Apple Pear Pie with Cheddar Crumble

A few years ago, we planted several pear trees out front, followed by two apple trees. After fortifying the pear trees against every critter here in the high desert, we got a nice crop of pears, so this pie recipe is a perfect way to use them (along with grilling). We limit the amount of sugar, let the fruit and spices take center stage. The cheese crumble really turns this pie into a comfort food!

Ingredients

Crumble:

- ½ cup all-purpose flour
- brown sugar
- ¾ cup cheddar cheese, grated
- ¼ cup nuts (pecans, walnuts, or hazelnuts)
- ¼ cup butter, grated or cut in small pieces

Pie:

- 1 prepared pie crust
- ¼ cup cane sugar or honey
- ¼ cup brown sugar
- 2 tbsp all-purpose flour
- 1 tsp cinnamon
- ¼ tsp ground ginger
- ¼ tsp ground nutmeg
- ¼ cup pecans
- 2 granny smith apples, cored, cut longwise in thin slices
- 2 Cosmic Crisp apples (or your favorite variety), cored, cut longwise in thin slices
- 4 pears, cored, cut longwise in thin slices
- 1 tbsp lemon juice

1. Preheat the oven to 400 °F and place the pie crust into a pie pan. Put the apple and pear slices in a bowl and toss with the lemon juice.
2. Combine the crumble ingredients in a bowl, stir with a fork until they start to clump.
3. In a small bowl, whisk the sugar, flour, cinnamon, ginger, nutmeg, and pecans for the pie filling, then add to the apples and pears and toss to combine.
4. Transfer the pie filling mixture with the apples and pears into the pie crust.
5. Pour the crumble on top of the pie filling creating an even layer.
6. Place the pie in the center of the oven with a cookie sheet underneath to catch any overflow drippings.
7. Bake the pie for about 45 minutes, until it is bubbly.
8. Let the pie rest for 15-30 minutes then serve. We like it warm along with a scoop of vanilla ice cream or homemade whipped cream.

Category Index

Kitchen Essentials
Baking Dishes, 9
Cast Iron Pans, 9
Cutting Boards, 8
Dutch Ovens, 9
Grill, 9
Hand/Emulsion Blender, 9
Knives, 8
Measuring Tools, 8
Meat Grinder, 9
Pizza Stone, 9
Pots And Pans, 9
Roasting Pan, 9
Rolling Mat, 9
Stand Mixers, 9
Thermometers, 8

The Basics
Beet Pickled Eggs, 19
Brandy Whipped Cream, 14
Chimichurri, 11
Crushed Chipotle in Adobo Sauce, 11
Fresno Pepper Hot Sauce, 11
Helen Rennie's Magic Sauce, 11
Homemade Stock, 17
Hot Sauces, 12
Johnson's Barbeque Sauce, 15
Mayonnaise and Aioles, 13
Mustard, 11
Oils, 12
Pickled Onions and Jalapenos, 20
Poached Eggs, 18
Revamped Russian Dressing, 16
Vinegars, 12
Wines, 11

Favorites
BJ's Capri Salad, 37
Cast Iron Stir Fry, 33
Creamed Chipped Beef (SOS), 36
Earthly Omelet, 30
Flightline Nachos, 31
Grandma Tate's Potato Pancakes, 25
High Desert Omelet, 27
Hilltop Haluski, 43
Leftover Steak Fajitas, 42
LO Rib and Pineapple Fajitas, 39
Mountain Guide's Reuben, 29
Pickled Grilled Cheese, 38
Pork Medallions and Plums, 34
Port Braised Beef Shanks, 35
Potato and Chorizo Crispy Tacos, 44
Saddle Butte Perogies, 40
South Street Perogies, 41
Southland French Toast, 26
The "E&A" Sandwich, 28
The All-Day BLT, 32
Waffle House Tribute, 45

On The Grill
Barbeque Smoked Salmon, 56
Brandy Marinated Grilled Pineapple, 50
Carolyn's Grilled Corn, 51
Grilled Country Style Ribs and Pineapple, 53
Grilled Ribeye Steak, 54
Juniper Grilled Game Hens, 52
Marinated Pork Chops with Plum Chutney, 57
Prospectors Burger, 47
Ranchhand Thin Burgers, 48-49
Smoked Duck Breast with Cherry Port Sauce, 55

Category Index

Hoagies and Sandwiches

Delaware and Oregon Special -
   Pork Roll Egg and Cheese, 60
Duke's Meatball Sandwich, 64
Front Street Steak Sandwich, 67
Garlic Chicken Cheese Steak, 63
Hot Roast Beef and Mozzarella Hoagie, 65
Phil's Pepperoni Pizza Steak, 68
Roast Beef and Fried Onion Hoagie, 62
Schuylkill Station Special -
   Scrapple Egg and Cheese, 61
Two Street Grinder, 59
Tailgate Tribute – Brats with Kraut, 66

Seafood

Cast Iron Barbeque Shrimp, 78
Cast Iron Dover Sole, 82
Chesapeake Fried Green Tomatoes-
   and Garlic Shrimp, 80
First Mates Crab Stuffed Shrimp, 71
Inner Harbor Crabcakes, 76
New Iberia Shrimp and Andouille, 72
Seared Garlic Shrimp Tacos, 77
Shrimp and Okra Hoagie, 79
The Queen's Fish and Chips, 81
Western Seared Scallops, 73
Xen Tuna Loin with Sushi Rice Blocks, 74-75

Pork Butt Bonanza

10th Street Roast Pork Sandwich, 86
8 Minute Egg Rolls, 94
Biscuits and Sausage Gravy, 91
BJ's Ground Pork, 85
Bourbon Pulled Pork, 95
JB's Meatballs and Red Sauce, 90
Lion's Head Meatballs and Leftovers, 87-88
Mountain View Meatloaf and Leftovers, 92-93
The Southwark: Sausage Egg and Cheese, 89

Hamamania

Bourbon Pulled Pork, 95
Grilled Ham and Avocado Sandwich, 99
Ham Bone Chowder, 104
Ham Egg and Cheese Hoagie, 98
Ham Mac and Cheese Fajita, 103
Ham Mac and Cheese Pizza, 102
Ham, Pickled Apple. And Onion Pizza, 100
Honey Mustard Chipotle Sauce, 97
Jalapeno Mac and Cheese with Ham, 101

Pizza and Pasta

Carolyn's Skillet Pasta Pie, 112-113
Catch All Calzones, 120
CJ's Traveling Lasagna, 118-119
Classic Style Napoli Pizza, 108
Green Tomato Pizza, 109
Leftover Pasta Refresh, 115
Make Ahead Pasta Sauce, 107
Oiled Spinach Mushroom Pasta, 114
Pizza and Calzone Dough, 106
Spanish Chorizo and Cotija Pizza, 111
Spinach and Garlic White Pizza, 110
Spinach and Mushroom Manicotti, 116
Summer Pasta Salad, 117

Chicken and Duck

Bar-B-Que Chicken Pizza, 127
Buffalo Barbeque Chicken Wings, 130
Buffalo Bar-B-Que Chicken Calzones, 129
Buffalo Blue Cheese Chicken Salad Hoagie, 128
Chicken Corn Okra Rice Hand Pies, 131
Chicken Two Ways-Fried, 123
Old Bay Chicken Corn Salad Sandwich, 125
Quick Chicken Fajitas, 126
Rendered Duck Fat, 134
Roasted Chicken with Cranberry Sauce, 122

Category Index

Sides

Barbeque Fried Brussels, 153

BJ's Duck Fat Potatoes, 138

Bobbi's Spinach and Pea Risotto, 148

Braised Green Beans, 154

Carolyn's Creamed Spinach, 155

CJ's Avocado Corn Salsa, 141

Classic Diner Home Fries, 158

Coconut Rice, 157

Desert Dirty Rice, 142

Drew's Roasted Carrots, 156

Edna's Fermented Cabbage Kraut, 136-137

Garden Vegetable Orzo, 152

Ginger Rice, 143

Grilled Baked Potato, 149

Honey Chipotle Apples and Onions, 145

Japanese Cucumber Salad, 151

Kathryn's Baked Beans, 139

Nordic Root Vegetable Mash, 147

Roasted Okra, 140

Russet and Sweet Potato Fries, 150

Vegetable Corn Rice, 144

Western Mushy Peas, 146

Desserts

Apple Pear Pie with Cheddar Crumble, 164

Bourbon Grilled Peaches, 162

Candied Pecans and Peanuts, 163

Cherry-Vanilla Clafoutis, 161

JB's Rice Pudding, 160

Recipe Index

A

Apple Pear Pie with Cheddar Crumble, 164

B

Barbeque Fried Brussels, 153
Barbeque Smoked Salmon, 56
Bar-B-Que Chicken Pizza, 127
Beet Pickled Eggs, 19
Biscuits and Sausage Gravy, 91
BJ's Capri Salad, 37
BJ's Duck Fat Potatoes, 138
BJ's Ground Pork, 85
Bobbi's Spinach and Pea Risotto, 148
Bourbon Grilled Peaches, 162
Bourbon Pulled Pork, 95
Braised Green Beans, 154
Brandy Marinated Grilled Pineapple, 50
Brandy Whipped Cream, 14
Buffalo Barbeque Chicken Wings, 130
Buffalo Bar-B-Que Chicken Calzones, 129
Buffalo Blue Cheese Chicken Salad Hoagie, 128

C

Candied Pecans and Peanuts, 163
Carolyn's Creamed Spinach, 155
Carolyn's Grilled Corn, 51
Carolyn's Skillet Pasta Pie, 112-113
Cast Iron Barbeque Shrimp, 78
Cast Iron Dover Sole, 82
Cast Iron Stir Fry, 33
Catch All Calzones, 120
Cherry-Vanilla Clafoutis, 161
Chesapeake Fried Green Tomatoes and Garlic-Shrimp, 80
Chicken Corn Okra Rice Hand Pies, 131
Chicken Two Ways-Fried, 123
CJ's Avocado Corn Salsa, 141

C

CJ's Traveling Lasagna, 118-119
Classic Diner Home Fries, 158
Classic Style Napoli Pizza, 108
Coconut Rice, 157
Creamed Chipped Beef (SOS), 36

D

Delaware and Oregon Special - Pork Roll Egg and Cheese, 60
Desert Dirty Rice, 142
Drew's Roasted Carrots, 156
Duke's Meatball Sandwich, 64

E

Earthly Omelet, 30
Edna's Fermented Cabbage Kraut, 136-137
8 Minute Egg Rolls, 94

F

First Mates Crab Stuffed Shrimp, 71
Flightline Nachos, 31
Front Street Steak Sandwich, 67

G

Garden Vegetable Orzo, 152
Garlic Chicken Cheese Steak, 63
Ginger Rice, 143
Grandma Tate's Potato Pancakes, 25
Green Tomato Pizza, 109
Grilled Baked Potato, 149
Grilled Country Style Ribs and Pineapple, 53
Grilled Ham and Avocado Sandwich, 99
Grilled Ribeye Steak, 54

H

Ham Bone Chowder, 104
Ham Egg and Cheese Hoagie, 98

Recipe Index

H
Ham Mac and Cheese Fajita, 103
Ham Mac and Cheese Pizza, 102
Ham, Pickled Apple. And Onion Pizza, 100
High Desert Omelet, 27
Hilltop Haluski, 43
Homemade Stock, 17
Honey Chipotle Apples and Onions, 145
Honey Mustard Chipotle Sauce, 97
Hot Roast Beef and Mozzarella Hoagie, 65

I
Inner Harbor Crabcakes, 76

J
Jalapeno Mac and Cheese with Ham, 101
Japanese Cucumber Salad, 151
JB's Meatballs and Red Sauce, 90
JB's Rice Pudding, 160
Johnson's Barbeque Sauce, 15
Juniper Grilled Game Hens, 52

K
Kathryn's Baked Beans, 139

L
Left Over Barbeque Rib Sandwich, 69
Leftover Pasta Refresh, 115
Leftover Steak Fajitas, 42
Lion's Head Meatballs and Leftovers, 87-88
LO Rib and Pineapple Fajitas, 39

M
Make Ahead Pasta Sauce, 107
Marinated Pork Chops with Plum Chutney, 57
Mayonnaise and Aioles, 13
Mountain Guide's Reuben, 29
Mountain View Meatloaf and Leftovers, 92-93

N
New Iberia Shrimp and Andouille, 72
Nordic Root Vegetable Mash, 147

O
Oiled Spinach Mushroom Pasta, 114
Old Bay Chicken Corn Salad Sandwich, 125

P
Phil's Pepperoni Pizza Steak, 68
Pickled Grilled Cheese, 38
Pickled Onions and Jalapenos, 20
Pizza and Calzone Dough, 106
Poached Eggs, 18
Pork Medallions and Plums, 34
Port Braised Beef Shanks, 35
Potato and Chorizo Crispy Tacos, 44
Prospectors Burger, 47

Q
Quick Chicken Fajitas, 126

R
Ranchhand Thin Burgers, 48-49
Rendered Duck Fat, 134
Revamped Russian Dressing, 16
Roast Beef and Fried Onion Hoagie, 62
Roasted Chicken with Cranberry Sauce, 122
Roasted Okra, 140
Russet and Sweet Potato Fries, 150

S
Saddle Butte Perogies, 40
Schuylkill Station Special - Scrapple Egg and- Cheese, 61
Seared Garlic Shrimp Tacos, 77
Seared Squid Steak, 83
Shrimp and Okra Hoagie, 79

Recipe Index

S

Smoked Duck Breast with Cherry Port Sauce, 55
South Street Perogies, 41
Southland French Toast, 26
Spanish Chorizo and Cotija Pizza, 111
Spinach and Garlic White Pizza, 110
Spinach and Mushroom Manicotti, 116
Summer Pasta Salad, 117

T

Tailgate Tribute – Brats with Kraut, 66
10th Street Roast Pork Sandwich, 86
The "E&A" Sandwich, 28
The All-Day BLT, 32
The Queen's Fish and Chips, 81
The Southwark: Sausage, Egg and Cheese Sandwich, 89
Two Street Grinder, 59

V

Vegetable Corn Rice, 144

W

Waffle House Tribute, 45
Western Mushy Peas, 146
Western Seared Scallops, 73

X

Xen Tuna Loin with Sushi Rice Blocks, 74-75